T5-DHV-383

As the original Immersion Traveler, I am thrilled to be included in Michael Schneider's great book that epitomizes the very best of immersion travel—connecting with people and places, getting involved, and giving back.

—Sheryl Kayne, author of *Immersion Travel USA* and *Volunteer Vacations across America*

One day I talked with Mike about how I wanted to spend time in Africa. Next thing I know I'm settled in Zimbabwe without spending a dime of my own money. Mike's guidance on locating overseas work is right on the mark, and his advice made it possible for me to spend three glorious months living and working overseas. I heartily encourage you to do the same.

—Paul Tymann, Professor and Chair, Department of Computer Science, Rochester Institute of Technology

Michael Schneider does what many of us want to do, but few ever manage—to live all over the world without giving up his house, job, or nest egg. And in *On the Other Guy's Dime* he shows you the practical steps needed to do it yourself.

—Christina Bolton, Editor, *inTravel Magazine,* www.intravelmag.com

Not only is this a great chronicle of places to see and experiences not to be missed, it's also an invaluable guide to finding the money to get there, stay there, and come back safely. What Michael Schneider reveals in this book is a journey into the richness of cultures and people unknown to most of us, and all "on the other guy's dime." Treat yourself to a real trip and buy this book."

–Sister Karol Jackowski, author of *Ten Fun Things to Do before You Die* and several other books

Michael's stories are fascinating and entertaining and offer a glimpse into the world of a traveler. However, he also provides practical tips and helpful hints for anyone interested in following in his footsteps.

–George Christodoulou, Editor, One Travel Blog. Onetravel.com

ON THE OTHER GUY'S DIME

A Professional's Guide to Traveling Without Paying

by G. Michael Schneider

Tasora

Copyright © 2010 by G. Michael Schneider

All rights reserved. No part of this publication may be
reproduced in any manner whatsoever without the prior written
permission of the publisher or author.

Printed in the United States of America on acid-free paper.

ISBN 978-1-934690-40-6

Cover design by Kyle G. Hunter
Interior design by Rachel Holscher
Design, typesetting, and printing by BookMobile

To order additional copies of this book, please go to:
www.itascabooks.com

Dedication

This book is dedicated to my son Benjamin, daughter Rebecca,
son-in-law Trevor, two dear grandchildren Liam and Sena,
and Ruthann, my wife and favorite traveling companion
with whom I have shared every adventure.

Travelers and tourists, the distinction is simple: Tourists are those who bring their homes with them wherever they go, and apply them to whatever they see. They are closed to experiences outside of the superficial. Travelers, however, leave home at home, bringing only themselves and a desire to learn.

—Gary Langer

Contents

Preface

I am an explorer with the heart and soul of a nomad. I love traveling to remote corners of the globe and living in unfamiliar surroundings, but I don't love shelling out the large sums needed to pay for my wanderlust. Fortunately, I've discovered a solution to this conundrum. I've been on more than a dozen overseas adventures, living and working for periods of one to eight months, never once reaching deeply into my wallet or giving up my day job.

These journeys have taken my wife Ruth and me to England, Israel, Kenya, Australia, Turkey, Japan, Zimbabwe, Mauritius, Malaysia, Nepal, Tibet, Mongolia, and Bhutan. We've gazed at Everest, ridden camels in the Gobi, walked with elephants in the Serengeti, and lived on a tropical island paradise—our expenses all happily and purposefully paid by someone else.

Life did not start out that way. At the age of thirty-five I had never ventured more than a few miles outside the United States. I was a comfortable and rather insular Midwestern college professor, first at the University of Minnesota and then a few miles down the road at Macalester College in St. Paul. Like many in my profession, I was content teaching classes, publishing papers, and attending a conference or two if money were available.

I enjoyed the pace of academic life, with the high intensity of teaching and research bracketed by recuperative periods called Thanksgiving, Christmas, spring break, and summer vacation. We don't earn anything close to our peers in the private sector, but as a tradeoff we're given time to recover, regenerate, and enjoy. Teaching is a great life, but I was to discover how much better it could be.

Until the middle of my third decade, I was totally unaware of the many opportunities available to academics, working professionals, and retirees to have others pay your way overseas during break periods such as sabbaticals, short-term leaves, and summer vacation. But I learned. Specifically, I learned about "working vacations" in which others fund your visit to their country to join them in teaching, consulting, or research at their home institution.

As I did more and more overseas work, I accumulated a wealth of practical experience and found out how to locate the best opportunities, negotiate terms of the visit, rent our home, find housing and transportation in the host country, and travel easily and safely with young children. Curious, not to mention jealous, colleagues started asking questions about how I was able to pull off these exotic trips, so I would relate my stories and explain how they could create their own adventures to their own dream destinations.

I often wondered why more academics, skilled professionals, and retirees, many with résumés and reputations far more impressive than mine, did not take advantage of these no-cost travel opportunities—and that is how this book was born. It is a travel memoir in which I share stories about our most memorable adventures and the lessons learned along the way. It is also a "how-to" guide intended to teach you the skills I have acquired over the years—the ability to locate and evaluate overseas work opportunities and the practical knowledge to turn that information into reality.

When I tell people where we have been and what we have seen over the past three decades, all at someone else's expense, they are convinced there must be something special about my education, field of study, or connection to private, state, and federal funding agencies. Believe me when I say I'm not special. I didn't graduate top of the class from Harvard or Oxford. I didn't bribe anyone to get what I wanted. I don't have friends in high places or an "in" that gets me past the velvet rope. The only thing I did differently is that instead of simply talking about my dreams, I acted on them. It's amazing how often good information and simple, direct action can lead to success—exactly the success you can achieve after reading this book.

I won't exhaustively detail every adventure my wife and I have been lucky enough to experience. My intent is not to overwhelm with exploits or impress with frequent flyer mileage. Instead, I want to rekindle that youthful passion for long-term travel and overseas adventure that might have taken you tramping around Europe, Asia, and Africa opening doors to different cultures and giving you a new outlook on the world, or ignite a passion that has yet to be indulged.

My goal is to share what I have accomplished and encourage you to try it yourself—to live and work abroad, have some fun and adventure, and grow professionally, culturally, and intellectually— all on someone else's dime.

CHAPTER 1

What's a Working Vacation Anyway?

What could be better than a one-week, one-month, or even a one-year vacation to some exotic, far-off locale? That's easy—having someone else pay for it. This sounds a bit cheeky, even a tad unsavory, but it's a realistic and attainable goal for high school, college, and university faculty, and other professionals including doctors, lawyers, engineers, artists, and business specialists who can apply for short-term, unpaid leaves of absence. It is also an attractive option for retirees healthy enough for long-term travel. I can personally attest to the validity of this assertion, having made more than a dozen overseas jaunts in the last three decades without once digging too deeply into my own wallet.

I don't mean getting a hotel room "comped" because you are losing at the craps table or having someone pick up a dinner tab while you suffer through a high-pressure sales pitch. I am referring to what I call a *working vacation*. Nothing mysterious about this; it is a well-known and highly popular employment option for new college graduates.

Every year tens of thousands of young men and women work

in the United States or overseas with the Peace Corps, VISTA, AmeriCorps, Teach For America, JET (Japanese Exchange and Teaching) or any number of non-profit exchange programs that send students and recent graduates off to every corner of the globe. These programs typically cover transportation costs and provide room and board for the duration of the overseas stay. In exchange, volunteers work in the host country, share their expertise with locals, and assist in such areas as sustainable agriculture, education, health care, sanitation, and human rights. These non-profit exchange programs offer a wonderful way for young men and women to combine long-term travel with a socially responsible job that pays enough to cover their basic expenses. This is what I mean by having someone else foot the bill for your adventures abroad.

However, the downside to overseas programs aimed primarily at the youth market is they often ask participants to adopt a spartan lifestyle with few of the creature comforts that most senior academics and mature professionals would want and expect. Accommodations can be minimal, perhaps a dormitory or shared room at a youth hostel, while living conditions—sanitation, diet, and personal safety—are often dicey. Furthermore, you must commit to the program for a relatively long period. For example, Peace Corps and Teach For America require a two-year sign-up, while VISTA demands a minimum one-year term.

So, although it sounds attractive to head out and see the world with someone else picking up the tab, a few modifications need to be made before the concept is fully palatable to those of us past the age of thirty and well past sleeping bags, shared toilets, and outdoor showers. What I am describing might be called a "Peace Corps-like experience for grown-ups."

What makes academics and professionals in their thirties, forties, fifties, and sixties (and beyond) different as a group from teens or twenty-somethings when it comes to working abroad? What makes programs for established adults distinct from those designed primarily for a younger audience? After all doesn't everyone, regardless of age, simply want to travel and have fun while doing some good work along the way?

While it is difficult to make broad, sweeping generalizations about such a large and diverse cohort as "mature academics," "experienced professionals," or "recent retirees," I think it is fair to say that as a group we share some or all of the following characteristics that distinguish us from younger volunteers:

1. Commitments. Unlike students who head off to Europe, Asia, or Africa and don't rush back (because it means finding a job, going to graduate school, or "settling down"), people in the thirty to seventy age bracket typically have deep community roots and significant family and work commitments that can make it difficult, if not impossible, to get away from home for a year or two at a time. A six-month stay may exceed their limit. Even retirees who, you might assume, have nothing but free time, may not want to leave home for an extended period because of family ties or health concerns. To consider an overseas working vacation most professionals require programs with a duration of from three to four weeks (any shorter and you might as well take a regular, non-working holiday) up to a maximum of one year. The most common block of time that can be freed up by those in private sector jobs or academic positions is two to six months—typically a summer vacation, one-semester sabbatical, or a short-term leave of absence.

2. Skill sets. Established professionals have honed and polished their skills to a high level. By comparison, programs such as the Peace Corps are aimed at recent graduates with little or no professional experience; volunteers often carry out a more limited range of tasks—small-scale farming, teaching ESL (English as a

Second Language), youth outreach, or community organizing. In contrast, working or retired professionals with Ph.D., Ed.D., M.D., D.D.S., J.D., M.B.A., M.Sc., or M.F.A. degrees are highly experienced and have attained success in any one of a number of skilled occupations. To entice these talented people to participate in an overseas program it must take full advantage of their sophisticated skills and provide numerous opportunities to use those skills in productive ways.

3. Families. Unlike students, many professional visitors arrive with a spouse and one or more children in tow. While living in a remote village far from the nearest health center might be something we considered in our youthful idealism and ignorance, most of us would hesitate to accept those same living arrangements when traveling with children. Being posted to a country with a long history of violence and discord might not scare off young nomads, but it would certainly be disconcerting to those of us with dependents. Overseas programs need to be located in a safe and stable environment and include appropriate schooling, health care, and recreational activities for families with children.

4. Expectations. Young people may be content simply to live and work in an exotic location, but most professionals and their families will not be lured into an overseas program by work experiences alone. While contributing to a developing economy and interacting with local experts may be of primary importance, senior academics and other skilled professionals will also expect ample opportunity to experience the culture, history, and natural beauty of their host country. In addition to work, they will want to sample the local attractions, whether it is shopping, hiking, snorkeling, horseback riding, wine tasting, or mountain climbing. A working vacation must provide adequate release time to allow its participants to take full advantage of what the host country and its region have to offer.

5. *Comfort Zones.* Finally, and perhaps of greatest importance, is that "grown-ups" at the peak of their professional lives want a significantly higher level of comfort than they had while bumming around Europe in their teens or twenties. They no longer travel with a backpack, student discount card, and $20 in their pocket. They don't dine on potato chips and pizza and crash for the night on someone's couch. Sharing a dormitory and bathroom with a dozen or so others will probably not motivate older professionals to consider a visit. Reasonable accommodations, personal safety, quality health care, public transportation, good sanitation, and access to healthy and tasty food are all of the utmost importance.

In summary, I am describing an overseas work experience similar to the Peace Corps but modified to make it more attractive to established professionals between thirty and seventy, and even beyond. Specifically, it would last a minimum of about one month up to a maximum of twelve months (with two to six months typical), make full use of high-level skills, and provide comfortable, safe living accommodations for participants and their families, all within an environment where work is intermixed with ample time for sightseeing. I plan to convince you that this type of working vacation is not only feasible but an ideal way to combine a paid job with adventure travel and a chance to live in and become part of an overseas community.

When we were eighteen to thirty years old many of us relished the idea of living, not just traveling, abroad. We dreamed of heading off to Europe after graduation (and a good number actually did) to experience a new culture and mature as young adults and global citizens. We had a zeal to be part of what Jews term *tikkun olam,* the repair of the world. We were not interested in a one-week "Highlights Tour" or a whirlwind dash past a few major tourist attractions. Instead we wanted to stay for a while, learn the language, and become part of the local community.

Why should that taste for adventure fade as we grow older? Why must we abandon our idealism and wanderlust because we are no longer twenty-something? Even though we have added a few years, a few dependents, and a few pounds, why aren't we still as passionate about combining the joy and excitement of living and working abroad with a desire to help others around the world?

When you live in a community, rather than drop in for a few days, there is sufficient time to meet neighbors, attend social, cultural, and religious events, and participate in local activities. Everyday tasks like shopping, laundry, even getting a haircut become your responsibility, not your tour guide's, and they require you to learn about the neighborhood and the people who live and work there. A long-term working vacation allows you to take those unusual but informative off-the-beaten-path excursions not possible in the jam-packed schedule of the typical one- or two-week family holiday. You learn about a culture not by observing it from a distance but by becoming part of it. In a recent book by Sheryl Kayne,[1] the author uses the term *immersion travel* to describe this very idea. An excellent turn of phrase, and one I wish I had coined. I did not, so I will leave it to her and continue to use the term *working vacation.*

One's own social and political orientation can be profoundly influenced by these working vacations as you not only expand your understanding of the world but also gain insights into what is happening here at home. As Mark Twain wrote in *Innocents Abroad,*

---

1. *Immersion Travel USA: The Best & Most Meaningful Volunteering, Living, and Learning Excursions,* (Countryman, 2008).

"Travel is fatal to prejudice, bigotry, and narrow-mindedness, and many of our people need it sorely."

Travel to countries with deep-seated religious strife makes you acutely aware of the terrible societal damage caused by our own homegrown zealots. Living in the midst of a culture struggling with racial or tribal hatreds sensitizes you to the hurt—physical and spiritual—arising from intolerance, bigotry, and segregation. Working in a developing nation whose economic policies exacerbate the gap between rich and poor opens one's eyes to the ugliness of greed and the shame of our own society's tolerance of poverty amidst widespread wealth.

For many professionals these transformative experiences are far more rewarding than a Caribbean cruise or baking somewhere on a beach. A long-term working vacation is a wonderful way to combine the relaxation of a holiday with the intellectual growth and excitement of interacting with and learning from local residents and professionals. And all this on the other guy's dime!

Joint travel/work opportunities are available to a wide range of academics including high school teachers, community and junior college instructors, and professors at four-year public and private universities. They are also open to retirees as well as professionals who can apply for and receive short-term leaves of absence from their current positions. Many of us know or have heard stories of physicians, veterinarians, and nurses who have assisted at overseas clinics; engineers and scientists who have consulted with foreign governments on infrastructure development; or musicians who have played with orchestras abroad. These are only a few examples of the wide range of skills in high demand at overseas institutions.

I am an academic and have been since 1974. Since authors write about what they know best, my stories and examples are drawn from the domain of the college and the classroom, but this does not mean the opportunities described in the following pages apply only to faculty. If you are not teaching then simply adapt my suggestions to your circumstances. If I talk about contacting a school, think about writing a hospital, museum, research institute, or government agency. When I refer to a department chair, this might translate into your managing director, head curator, or conductor. The essence of the idea is the same, and the joy that comes from participating in a long-term overseas working vacation will be identical.

Many of the personal, cultural, and professional benefits of working vacations are also available in a quite different format called *volunteer tourism*. There are many different types of overseas volunteer opportunities but they frequently combine a bit of traditional vacation, such as a stay at a beach resort, followed by volunteer work in the same country or region helping out in whatever way you can. This is a wonderful and socially responsible form of travel but very different from the working vacation concept I am advocating.

Volunteer positions are often much briefer, usually a week or two, compared with the two- to six-month duration of the typical working vacation. Volunteer tourism obviously implies you will be working without pay; in fact, not only will you be unpaid, but you often have to lay out a significant sum to the agency arranging the volunteer visit, sometimes thousands of dollars, to cover the costs of trip planning, housing, insurance, and in-country staff.

Many people cannot afford to take an unpaid leave of absence for a significant length of time without being compensated for their efforts. In the following chapters I will be addressing overseas employment that pays enough to cover most or all of one's living and transportation expenses. However, Chapter 14 contains links to Web sites with information about volunteer tourism postings.

There is one final admonition that must be fully aired and discussed before diving into the details of planning a working vacation. Even though it may be a single professional in the family applying for the position, it is the *entire* family who will go, including a spouse or partner. If you are married or in a committed long-term relationship, it is critical that this individual be a supportive and enthusiastic ally, not an unhappy, unwilling participant in your adventure. It is unfair, not to mention very unpleasant, to spend months on an overseas trip in which you have no stake and absolutely no interest.

Remember when you were dragged kicking and screaming to that ballet, opera, or football game? In that case your agony lasted only a few hours and was soon forgotten. Now imagine the discomfort of attending an event that lasts three or six months! This is a recipe guaranteed to produce unhappiness and marital discord. (Unhappy kids are a different issue that I address in Chapter 4.)

So, before diving into the following chapters and eagerly sending off your application for a position in Portugal, Panama, or Papua New Guinea, be absolutely sure that both you and your life partner are enthusiastic about this undertaking and equally excited about the adventures that await. If that is the case then read on, and make certain your passports are up-to-date.

CHAPTER 2

My London Epiphany

Morris and Jeff were simply two faces among thousands attending the annual convention of computer science teachers in Dayton, Ohio. There was nothing particularly notable about either, save their thick "Monty Pythonesque" British accents. Today, with world travel the norm and BBC-TV on virtually every cable system, this wouldn't be worth a mention or even a turn of the head. However, in spring 1979 in the insular heartland of the United States, it was an oddity that caught my attention. I sat down beside them at lunch, exchanging pleasantries, to learn they were computer science faculty at Imperial College, London, working in the same area of teaching and research as I—the design and verification of computer network protocols. Our lunchtime conversation was most enjoyable and advanced to the point of exchanging business cards and making the perfunctory promise to "keep in touch." Little did I imagine the significance of those throwaway words.

Six months later, in fall 1979, I received a long-distance telephone call from Morris—this was many years ago so e-mail and faxes were not yet ubiquitous. He had received a research grant from the British Computing Society that included financial support for a visiting international scholar. He remembered our lunchtime chat, managed to unearth my business card from the clutter on his desk, and invited me to join him in London for three months the following summer. The grant would provide airfare, housing allowance, and a modest stipend sufficient to cover our family's daily living expenses. I would need to pay only the cost of air tickets for my wife and children.

The proposed dates meshed perfectly with the summer vacation schedule at my school, the University of Minnesota, so no problem, right? Well maybe not for an experienced traveler comfortable with heading overseas at the drop of an invitation, but Morris' offer was made to someone thirty-four years of age who had never ventured more than ten miles beyond the borders of the continental United States—specifically, to Windsor, Ontario; and Tijuana, Mexico. The idea of *going* to London was a lot for me to digest; the thought of *living* there for the entire summer was overwhelming and, to be honest, rather scary. I had a wife and two young children (nine and six at the time), a home, two cars, a lawn and garden. I was in a bowling league and played poker every Monday night. You can't just pick up and leave such pressing responsibilities behind. Or can you?

My fears kicked into high gear and I began to spew out dozens of reasons why this preposterous and foolhardy idea could not possibly work. Who would care for the house in our absence? What about my quest for tenure? How would we pay the bills? How could we disrupt the kids' lives? What about Aunt Edith's seventieth birthday party next July? My wife, far more footloose and adventurous than I (she had traveled to Europe on her own for two months the year before we were married) had a simple rejoinder for each concern: We can rent the house to responsible adults; Imperial College is a world-class school ranked alongside

Oxford and Cambridge, so any scholarly work you do there will certainly contribute to tenure; the kids can play with each other and will quickly make friends in the neighborhood; we can call Aunt Edith on her birthday. All her arguments were thoughtful, reasonable, and logical, but in the end only one truly swayed me: "Dammit, this will be an adventure. Let's do it!"

That pithy and spot-on comment did the trick, and on May 18, 1980, the Schneider clan headed to the Minneapolis airport to board a flight to the British Isles. We had rented our house to our neighbor's sister and brother-in-law coming to Minneapolis from New Zealand for three months. (They obviously did not have as many qualms about travel as I did.) They promised to forward our mail, mow the lawn, and pay the mortgage. However, our neighbor's brother-in-law hated bowling and poker, so my teammates and poker buddies would have to find another replacement for me for a few months.

The house that our English hosts had rented for us was a 120-year old three-bedroom Georgian in the quaint, middle-class suburb of Chiswick in SW London, an easy commute via the Underground to my office in South Kensington. While decidedly trendier and more upscale today, in 1980 the neighborhood had few tourists, no boutique shopping, and no cutting-edge fusion restaurants. It was a lovely area of teachers, bus drivers, salesmen, and pensioners. I had to admit that, so far, there had been no problems, and my wife's arguments in support of coming to England were holding up surprisingly well.

We quickly made friends with colleagues at work and were soon invited to dinners, movies, and parties. To repay their many kindnesses we threw a Fourth of July BBQ bash at our home complete with red, white, and blue streamers; hamburgers; potato salad; and a build-your-own banana split bar. It was a huge success as it seemed that my Imperial College colleagues were just as eager to learn about American customs and traditions as I was to learn about theirs. The kids played in the local park, met neighbor children, and, as so often happens, this led to our meeting their parents, adding more names to our growing London social directory. We attended a nearby synagogue for Saturday morning services, were introduced to congregants, and in a short time became part of the local Jewish community. Our relatives, knowing they had a comfortable (and free) place to stay, not to mention an "experienced guide" to show them the city, came for extended visits, further choking our already-packed dance card.

In fact, one of the travel skills I have never been able to master, even after thirty years, is the ability to say no to friends, colleagues, or family members when they ask to stay with us for a week or more. Just as I enjoy traveling on the other guy's dime so do others, especially with regard to free accommodations in expensive and highly desirable locations like London, Paris, or Tuscany. So, be forewarned. If your working vacation takes you to one of these popular and pricey tourist destinations, be prepared to play host to high school buddies, college roommates, down-the-block neighbors, and second cousins once removed. Either that or learn to do what I never could—look them directly in the eye and say, "I'm sorry, but no."

Although England is not exactly an alien culture to Americans, my wife and I were experiencing new ways of doing things daily. We learned to shop like Brits—instead of the one-stop "Gonzo-Mart" for all our food needs, we hauled our reusable straw bags (a new concept in the pre-green days of 1980) to the neighborhood butcher, greengrocer, fishmonger, baker, and dairy shop. We chowed down on great Indian and Pakistani cuisine, common in London (their equivalent of neighborhood Chinese) but a rarity in 1980s Minneapolis.

Born and raised in Detroit, I considered the automobile an extension of the human body, as indispensable as your nose or right arm, and my definition of an efficient transit system was an eight-lane freeway. I worried that without access to a car we would be tied down to our immediate area. New Yorkers may laugh at this totally irrational concern, but coming from subway-less Minnesota it was not an unexpected misgiving. It took only a few days to learn that in this city a car was an unnecessary luxury and to appreciate the joys of a superb urban mass transit system. I mastered the brown, red, yellow, green, blue, pink, gray, and black lines of the Underground to such an extent that I was able to provide helpful advice not only to lost tourists but wandering locals as well.

With three months, rather than three days or three weeks, to explore this sprawling metropolis we had time to see not only the "biggies" of the English tourist scene—the British Museum, Hyde Park, Kew Gardens, Tower Bridge, and the Royal Observatory—but also to discover some oft overlooked sites and hidden gems, such as the British Postal Museum and Archives in Islington and the quirky but fascinating Fan Museum in Greenwich with its collection of over four thousand fans, some dating to the tenth century.

We had time to leisurely stroll through interesting neighborhoods like Brixton, home to London's African-Caribbean community; visit the antiquarian bookstores of Bloomsbury; watch the street performers in Covent Garden; and experience the trendy and tacky sights of Soho. There were also days when we would not go anywhere but, instead, stay home, read a book, play board games with the kids, watch the telly, and head off to bed at an early hour. This relaxed pace of sightseeing is one of the great benefits of an extended working vacation, and leads to a far more manageable life-style than the all-day, every-day hustle and bustle of the typical family holiday.

After almost three and a half months overflowing with new friendships and fascinating experiences, it was hard to accept that August 26, our scheduled departure date from London, had arrived. What once seemed like eons in the future had passed as quickly as an afternoon nap, and the rounds of good-bye parties and send-off events were bittersweet. In that brief span of time we had made close friends with whom we are still in contact; learned to live, shop, eat, and drink like a Brit; grown comfortable being on the "wrong side" of the road, and begun to think of London as our second home.

When we returned to our "first" home in Minneapolis, which was in perfect shape and spotlessly clean I might add, I asked myself why I had waited until I was thirty-five to attempt something like this. My accounting of income and expenses for the trip, completed for tax purposes the following April, showed that this three-month English adventure for a family of four had cost a grand total of $1,500 in out-of-pocket expenses, about $3,800 in today's dollars. The stay in London had been a break-even proposition, perhaps even generating a small surplus due to my Imperial College allowance and the rental income from our home in the United States. The additional out-of-pocket costs were due to unplanned, spontaneous family jaunts to Paris, the Lake District, Scotland, Devon, and the Cotswolds. We could only marvel at how many things we had seen and how well we had lived over the past three months at a cost that would probably not cover a two-week stay for a family of four at an upscale Caribbean resort.

Making it even more lucrative was my discovery, late on the night of April 14, of the "Temporary Job Away From Home" tax deduction—an IRS fine point I was totally unaware of and had never before used. If you work overseas for less than one year with the expectation of returning home upon completion of the assignment—the very definition of a working vacation—you are allowed to deduct the cost of your airline tickets, housing, and a per diem amount for meals and incidental expenses, called M&IE in the tax tables. This can lead to a huge tax deduction with the potential for offsetting much of your working-vacation income and a significant chunk of regular salary.[2] For example, the current M&IE per diem rate for London, England, as set by the U.S. State Department, aoprals.state.gov/web920/per_diem.asp, is $140/day. If you were to work for the identical 105-day period that we did, this would result in a tax deduction of $14,700 for just meals and incidentals, not even including air transportation. This deduction is a wonderful way to have fun living and working overseas with Uncle Sam picking up a portion of the tab.

Not only was the trip a financial success, it was a professional and personal success as well. As part of a skilled research team, I learned a great deal from Morris and Jeff and was able to initiate scholarly activities that laid the groundwork for two future publications. Just as my wife had said—and how I hate it when she is right—these articles did help me achieve tenure a few years later. My children had the opportunity to live in a different culture and play with British children raised in far different circumstances, and although they are now grown adults they still fondly remember that first overseas summer in England. All my imagined problems were just that; not a single one of my deep-seated worries had come to pass. I could think of nothing I would have changed except, perhaps, to host fewer houseguests.

Most important to me is that in those three plus months I started my transformation from someone who had grown far too comfortable with his familiar surroundings into, if not yet an experienced world traveler, at least someone open to new experiences and no longer afraid to venture beyond self-imposed boundaries. I began to understand that this no-cost working vacation to England was not a once-in-a-lifetime adventure that came about because of a fortuitous lunchtime conversation or miraculous

---

2. I am not a CPA, so check with your tax preparer or read about this deduction in a good tax manual before entering the numbers on your Form 1040. I don't think the IRS will accept the argument "But Schneider said . . ." as valid proof.

alignment of stars, and it did not happen because I am a unique individual with one-of-a-kind skills available nowhere else. For me this realization was an epiphany.

At the time, I was a young, unheralded computer science teacher not long removed from graduate school. However, 1980 was the beginning of the Internet age and people were talking about how it was changing commerce, education, and personal communication. With blind luck and incredible timing, I had elected to work in a field exploding with new developments and applications. This knowledge, even though I was not alone in possessing it, could be useful to not only Imperial College but dozens of schools around the world and, with a little bit of effort, I should be able to locate other opportunities to combine work and travel, mix professional and cultural experiences, and both contribute to and learn from others. What is so stunningly obvious today—that I possess useful skills of sufficient interest to institutions abroad that they would pay me to live and work in their country—struck like a thunderbolt thirty years ago. I was determined not to let three decades pass before my next overseas experience.

My goal is for you to have that same epiphany—to realize that living and working overseas is a doable, affordable, enjoyable, and intellectually exhilarating experience whether for a month or a year; whether teaching, engaging in research, or consulting; whether in Asia, Africa, Europe, or the Americas; with or without family. You don't need to be a superstar to take advantage of these opportunities, and you don't have to be in computing. Institutions around the world are eager to welcome and host professionals in a range of fields, including business, infrastructure development, genetics, women's rights, constitutional law, family medicine, urban transit, community theater, and conflict resolution, to name but a few. You need to immediately discard the mistaken belief that you have neither the résumé nor the reputation to apply for and secure an overseas teaching, consulting, or research position. What is most important is not your pedigree or field of specialization but a sense of adventure and a willingness to open your mind to the possibility of a short-term sojourn in a new locale.

I know that right now many of you are probably doing exactly what I did after receiving that initial call from Morris—conjuring up a gremlin's litany of worries, doubts, and problems. You are convincing yourself that, although I was able to pull off this overseas adventure, your situation is totally different, and it would be impossible for you and/or your family to get away this year and, most likely, the next. After all, there is your elderly mother; the kid who attends Camp Potowotamie; pruning the roses; coaching the soccer team; teaching summer school.

One thing I have learned during my travels is that there is never a shortage of reasons to explain why a chance can't be grabbed, an opportunity can't be seized, or an experience can't be lived. I would never dream of attempting a rejoinder to each and every excuse you might present. Instead, I simply paraphrase my wife's final and most persuasive argument made to me all those many years ago: "Dammit, it *was* an adventure. You *should* go!"

CHAPTER 3

Making Aliyah

It was not three decades until our next overseas work experience, just three years, and it didn't come about because of some fortuitous lunchtime chitchat but rather a small and somewhat insignificant article on page twenty of the *Chronicle of Higher Education,* a newspaper published exclusively for college faculty and administrators. It was fall 1982 and I was sitting in my office glancing through the current issue when I happened upon a story about teaching shortages at Israeli universities.

All able-bodied Israeli men and women, except the *Haredi,* ultra-Orthodox Jews, serve either two years (women) or three years (men) in the Israeli Defense Forces. Following active duty they are placed in the reserves until age fifty-one and may be called up for a maximum of thirty-nine days each year. Faculty who have completed their regular tour of duty often meet this reserve responsibility during summer when regular school is not in session.

The article went on to describe the problem Israeli universities were having offering summer classes since more than half their staff were serving in the armed forces. The shortages were especially acute in such high-demand areas as engineering, medicine, business, and *computer science* (emphasis mine). College administrators were encouraging English-speaking faculty, since most technical subjects are taught in English, to work in Israel for two or three months during the summer to help solve their problem.

Light bulbs popped! Trumpets blared! This article may have appeared in a national newspaper read by thousands, but I had no doubt it was speaking directly to me. It had been more than two years since our return from England, eyes newly opened to the world and eager to set off once more for points far and wide. However, rather than aggressively pursuing new opportunities, I had slipped into a holding pattern of work, family visits, and a week or two at a national park.

I knew what the problem was. The London trip had fallen into my lap. It had appeared out of the blue without any effort on my part, if you don't count that lunchtime conversation with Morris. The phone rang and from that point on everything was delivered on a platter like room service at a fine Manhattan hotel. Since our return I had assumed lightning would strike a second time; I was sitting back and waiting for a call offering me an all-expense-paid working vacation in some far-off locale. Well, in two years the phone hadn't rung and no offers were forthcoming, so instead I worked, bowled, and played poker. I was getting lazy and comfortable. Dreams about exotic destinations were becoming less frequent. I rarely took out our London scrapbook, and my kids, now twelve and nine, would soon become teenagers when traveling with parents would be viewed as a punishment worse than being grounded on prom night.

Then the *Chronicle* article appeared, personally inviting me to Israel for the summer. OK, it was inviting anyone in the English-speaking world who fogged a mirror and could teach at the university level, but in my gut I knew it was speaking to me. It sounded like a wonderful opportunity, but there was one small hitch. Unlike London, this time there would be no host holding our hands and smoothing the way, no colleagues who saw it as their responsibility to watch over us and help us with any difficulties that might arise. This offer was for a job, plain and simple. It would pay a salary and I would teach a class. Everything else—finding a place to live, getting acclimated to new surroundings, locating transport to school—would be my responsibility.

I showed the article to my wife who was ready to dig out her passport and start packing that evening. She felt a similar malaise—filled with unsatisfied wanderlust, ready to head off overseas but going nowhere. Israel was particularly attractive as a working destination because of our heritage. Most Jews dream of going to Israel at least once in their lifetime, much as an Irish-American hopes to walk the hallowed sod of County Galway or Korean-Americans might wish to see the homeland of their ancestors. Teaching in Israel would be an opportunity for my family to spend months getting to know the country and its people instead of simply whizzing past a few major tourist attractions—Masada, the Old City, the Dead Sea Scrolls—for a week or two.

Since all universities in Israel were suffering staff shortages, I was able to choose where I wanted to go. We decided on Hebrew University in Jerusalem, not because it has the strongest computer science program—that would be the Technion in Haifa—but because Jerusalem has the greatest historical, cultural, and religious heritage of any place in the country and is the one city in Israel that would offer us the greatest intellectual stimulation. When planning a working vacation it is important that your destination be sufficiently rich in scenic, cultural, social, and historical attractions to keep you mentally and physically occupied for the duration of the trip, a problem we were to experience firsthand during our residence, years later, in Ulan Bator, Mongolia.

I e-mailed the chair of computer science at Hebrew University (note the difference a few years made with regard to electronic communication), described my credentials and experience, provided the names of professional references, and listed the courses I was qualified to teach. In what seemed like only a few short moments after hitting SEND I received a formal invitation, although my memory must be playing tricks. There is a seven-hour time difference between Minneapolis and Jerusalem so my message would have arrived late at night. His response was terse, unemotional, and direct:

> You are hired and will be paid $X for teaching course Y as well as $Z in travel reimbursement. Please come to the Computer Science Department office on the *Givat Ram* campus of Hebrew University in Jerusalem on the morning of June 5, 1983. My secretary will e-mail you the room number and class meeting time. You can sign your contract when you arrive. Thank you and good-bye.

So much for "I'll meet you at the airport," "Let me help you find a place to live," or even "I cannot wait to meet you." However, unknown at the time, Israel turned out to be the perfect second working vacation. It allowed my wife and me to develop the "street smarts" needed to handle overseas travel on our own, without the crutch of a helpful and willing host to smooth over whatever bumps might occur.

People may laugh at this naiveté, but in 1983 moving from Minnesota to the Middle East for three months was not a trivial undertaking for a couple with two young children and precious little travel experience. The offer of a helping hand would have been deeply appreciated and graciously accepted, but there was none. We would have to learn to make do on our own, and in the future my wife and I would venture to remote destinations in much the same way—with a university and faculty eager to hire us but much too busy to act as our guide and mentor. Our stay in Israel taught us a great deal about self-sufficiency and self-confidence in a foreign country.

That trip also taught us about the benefits of a *summer* working vacation when traveling with school-age children. It is often the case that the local public school in the host country is inappropriate for your kids, perhaps because of overcrowding, a poor educational program or, in the case of Israel, the language of instruction—Hebrew—which my children did not speak very well. Finding a good English-language private school is rarely a problem as virtually every country in the world supports British, Australian, or American private schools that provide high-quality programs, usually for the children of wealthy businessmen, diplomats, and government employees. The issue is not one of availability but cost, since these schools often charge as much as their private counterparts back home.

For example, the Jerusalem American International School is a secular K-6 school with a superb educational program, set on a beautifully landscaped campus filled with gardens and fountains, but the annual tuition is $11,650 per student, along with a one-time registration fee of $1,500. Ouch! That kind of bill can shift the cost of a working vacation from the other guy's dime right into your own pocket. Unless you are traveling on a grant that covers the full cost of private education, such as the Fulbright grant described in Chapter 8, a summer working vacation can save you a lot of money as well as give you the flexibility to sightsee when you want, not just when school is out of session. You might wish to save those longer working vacations (six to twelve months) for when your children are grown and out of the house.

We rented our house in Minneapolis to a most unusual individual—a retired purveyor of "adult literature." Before there was such a thing as the World Wide Web, pornography was sold in sleazy bookstores filled with grizzled old men in trench coats and the scent of sweat and urine. Our renter owned such a place but had passed on operation of the business to his son when he moved into a retirement community in Phoenix. Arizona can be an unforgiving place in June, July, and August, so he would move back to Minnesota for the summer and find a place to live. Perfect for us, although it left our friends and family shocked and convinced that the house would look like a Pigalle bordello when we returned. I am happy to report that our porno grandpa was, without a doubt, the most responsible renter we've had in three decades of travel, and he ended up living in our home two additional times.

Finding good quality tenants to live in your home while you travel is not difficult, and it is an excellent way to generate income to help balance the books or cover the unexpected cost of spur-of-the-moment side trips. If your city is home to a medium- or large-sized college or university, like the University of Minnesota in Minneapolis, there will almost certainly be a university housing office providing online rental information to students, faculty, and, most importantly from our perspective, temporary visitors coming for summer or one-semester stays.

The cost of posting your home on these university databases is usually nominal, about $50–75. Large universities typically have hundreds of visitors flowing in and out of campus each semester, so it is the best way to reach the greatest number of potential renters whose arrival and departure dates mesh most closely with yours. Be sure to list your house at least three to four months in advance of departure to allow as much time as possible to reach these individuals. Our Arizona retiree learned about our house from a grandson who attends the university and searched their listings on behalf of his elderly relative.

There are other online rental sites that post information about temporary housing. The largest and most well known is craigslist, www.craigslist.org, which includes a specific category entitled "sublets/temporary housing" for hundreds of cities in the United

States and Canada and, best of all, this posting is free. (If you do use craigslist be prepared for an onslaught of e-mails from scammers eager to send a rental deposit as soon as you provide them with your bank account and Social Security number. Before posting or answering an ad check out the helpful advice on personal safety and scammers at http://www.craigslist.org/about/scams.) Another popular rental database is sabbaticalhomes.com, which focuses on the housing needs of academics coming to a city for a one-semester or one-year sabbatical visit. It includes information not only on home rentals, but home exchanges and house-sitting services as well.

Another possibility is to identify cultural institutions and corporate headquarters in your hometown that bring in professionals for short-term visits. For example, Minneapolis is home to the Minnesota Symphony Orchestra, the Guthrie Theater, and the Walker Art Center as well as the world or regional headquarters for 3M, Honeywell, Medtronic, and Northwest Airlines (now part of Delta), and at one time or another we have listed our home with all these institutions. One summer we rented to a guest conductor in town for "Sommerfest," our local summer music festival. Another time we rented to a visiting engineer from Australia working at the Honeywell Research Center. So, although it may take some telephone and computer work on your part, it should not be a great deal of trouble to locate a quality renter to live in and care for your home. Finally, after doing all this legwork, remember to carefully file away all those names, phone numbers, e-mail addresses, and Web sites for future reference. You really don't want to repeat the process from scratch when planning your second (and third and . . .) overseas working vacation.

For some people, having strangers live in their home while they are thousands of miles away is a nerve-racking thought, especially the first time. They worry incessantly about what the place will look like when they return—a worry that can end up detracting from their enjoyment. My advice is *don't*. Put away the valuables, antiques, and breakables. Have a friend stop by the house once a week or so to check in. Provide the names of handymen who can come on short notice if there is a problem. Then forget about the house while you focus on settling into your new life overseas. Besides, isn't that why they invented security deposits and home-owners insurance policies anyway?

So, with house rented, teaching contract in hand, and air tickets tucked safely into our pockets, on June 1, 1983, we found ourselves at the international terminal of Minneapolis-St. Paul airport for the first time in three years as we boarded a plane for Ben Gurion Airport, Tel Aviv. We landed twenty hours later, including a long layover in Amsterdam. I made a mental note that if I anticipated future long-distance air trips I needed to lay in a good supply of masks, earplugs, and sleep aids. With no one to meet us at the airport, the first noticeable difference between this trip and London, we took a jitney to Jerusalem and rented a room at a small hotel to tide us over until we found a place to live—the immediate task at hand.

If on-campus housing is not being provided, how do you locate an apartment in an unfamiliar country? Sometimes your hosts will make arrangements for a local realtor to come to the hotel on your first or second day in town, drive you around, and show you what is available. If this has not been proffered, send an e-mail message to your hosts asking them to arrange such an appointment. Then e-mail the realtor with your exact rental dates and the size unit you need so you will be shown only appropriate places.

Unfortunately, because of our limited travel experience, we had not done that. Instead, we dug out the Jerusalem Yellow Pages, which was printed in both Hebrew and English, looked under Real Estate, and jotted down the names of three or four agencies. I pre-paid a taxi to *schlep* us from place to place and wait while we talked with each realtor, a pricey but necessary luxury if we wanted to find something quickly. As it turned out, the driver was grossly overpaid as the first agent had something available for exactly the dates we needed. This was not a coincidence since the owners were Hebrew University faculty making the reverse commute—traveling to the United States for a summer work experience, and in the neighboring state of Wisconsin to boot.

The place was currently empty, as they had left the week before, so our transport vehicle morphed from a taxi into a delivery van as we reclaimed our belongings from the hotel and moved into new quarters, a lovely two-bedroom apartment in a ten-story building on *Derech Bet Lechem,* or Bethlehem Street for those like myself unfamiliar with Hebrew, one of the country's two official languages, Arabic being the other.

In fact, this impairment, my inability to speak conversational Hebrew, would be our first "welcome to Israel" moment as we discovered that not a single soul in our building either spoke English or was willing to try, while my Hebrew was limited to chanting prayers at Saturday morning services. (Hard to get a dialogue going when all you can say is "Blessed are thou o' Lord our God . . .") There were quite a few kids in the area but, like their parents, none were either able to speak or wanted to speak English with our children.

According to Israeli law English is a "semi-official" language, but it is widely spoken and understood, especially at universities (I would teach in English) and within the tourist sector—hotels, restaurants, shops, museums, and historical sites. Sadly, though, this list did not include our neighbors, grocery clerks, bus drivers, or apartment super. I quickly became expert at smiling, gesturing, and saying *"rega, rega"* (wait a minute) as I looked up a Hebrew phrase in my ever-present Berlitz guide. This was good training for future trips to Mongolia, Cambodia, and Ecuador where, outside the main tourist haunts, English fluency can be a rare bird.

It is a good idea, not to mention common courtesy, to learn at least a few helpful phrases in the local language, as I have done with Spanish, Bahasa Malaysia, Mongolian, and Japanese, and my children have done with French, and Mandarin Chinese. In fact, one of my earliest discoveries was that a language class is one of the best ways, along with reading country histories and travel guides, of preparing for an upcoming trip. This is particularly easy if you are an academic and your school teaches courses in that language. Simply walk into the classroom on the first day and ask if you can join, as I have done on a number of occasions.

Even if you are not working at a school it is still easy to learn the rudiments of a language—words like hello, goodbye, please, thank you, excuse me, how much, etc. Sign up for a community education class in your city or, if that is unavailable, buy a good computer-based language tutorial program such as Rosetta Stone. Then don't be afraid to use your admittedly limited language skills whenever possible. Whatever embarrassment might result from your butchering of the local tongue is more than made up for by the sincere appreciation of locals who will smother you with overblown compliments about how well you speak their language.

My second "welcome to Israel" moment occurred when I arrived at the computer science building two days before classes were to begin. I was given the key to my office and went there to store my books and teaching materials. However, the secretary had handed me the wrong key so I left the boxes by the door while I went to retrieve the proper one. When I returned, not five minutes later, I was accosted by two beefy security guards bellowing and pointing to what they called *chavilah chashudah,* suspicious package in English, and deciding whether or not to call the bomb squad. Sadly, after 9/11 the possibility of hidden explosives is no longer a rarity, and we are all familiar with metal detectors, warning announcements, and orange threat levels. But in 1983 this development was unexpected and highly disconcerting, and it took my pleas of newly arrived ignorance to assure the guards that the assemblage in front of the door was nothing more than textbooks and lecture notes.

After the guards had been convinced of the harmless nature of the boxes, I settled into the office and then wandered through the building hoping to meet colleagues. No such luck as the halls were empty. I knew I had been hired because of staff shortages, but I did not expect to see acres of deserted space and long corridors of empty rooms and locked doors. It felt like an office tower after closing, not a university building two days before the start of the summer semester. Were the people not on military duty off seeing the world? I met a sixty-something Israeli emeritus professor as well as two other Americans and one Canadian. That was it.

I took stock and realized how different this second working holiday was going to be compared with our first: no colleagues to welcome us and plan fun-filled parties in the backyard; no neighbors inviting us to dinner and a movie; no local kids romping with ours, playing games and sharing stories. I nervously asked myself if I had made a mistake. Had my dream of an ideal all-expenses-paid working vacation been pie-in-the-sky Pollyannaish optimism? Was this going to be the experience that proved my ideas about traveling on the other guy's dime wrong? Fortunately the ultimate answer to these nagging doubts and fears was a resounding "No!"

The situation we experienced in England, while enormously enjoyable and thoroughly satisfying, had been an anomaly. Deferential hosts and locals eager to bring you into their community are more the exception than the rule. Having someone on-site to find housing, rent a car, and point out the best hardware stores, grocery shops, and ethnic restaurants is an unexpected plus. More often than not your hosts will be excited to work with you and pleased with your contribution to their program but far too busy to act as mentors and guides. Your colleagues will offer helpful advice about places to live, where to eat, and the best sights to see, but they may leave you on your own to implement their suggestions. In rare instances neighbors will roll out the welcome wagon and become an everyday part of your overseas life. However, it is more likely that they will be polite, hospitable, and practically invisible.

We learned that, just as at home, good friendships do not happen automatically because of proximity—you live next door, you work in the same office. Instead, close friendships grow from mutual, shared interests. If you become active in the local community, in whatever manner you choose, you will meet people and make friends naturally rather than having it be assumed and forced.

My wife and I attended religious services at a *Masorti* synagogue, the Israeli term for Conservative Judaism, and met a few local congregants. We went to the nearby community swimming pool, listened for English conversations and, if we heard any, would introduce ourselves. Ironically, we met someone who graduated with me from high school and had made *aliyah,* emigration to Israel, ten years earlier and became our good friend for the duration of the stay. My wife had the name of a distant cousin we contacted and with whom we spent a good deal of time. On Saturday afternoon, when nothing in Jerusalem is open because of the Jewish Sabbath, we would go on English-language walking tours of the city and meet fellow walkers. This approach to making friends is no different from what we all must do when moving to a new city—the only difference being that we had only three months, not years, to establish these friendships, so we had to move quickly.

Eventually, we did meet some locals who exposed us to the joys and problems of life in Israel, including what it is like living in a country surrounded by enemies and in a perpetual state of conflict. While we were never directly touched by the ugliness and horror of terrorism, its reminders were constantly in view.

Soldiers in full battle gear carrying Uzi machine guns patrolled streets, buses, rail stations, and shopping malls. Any unattended package, as I had discovered earlier, would quickly be cordoned off by SWAT teams and examined by remote control. Every public building, including the computer center where I worked, had a shelter reminiscent of the underground bomb shelters that proliferated in the United States during the Cold War tensions of the 1950s and 60s.

The most compelling problem we encountered was not terrorism, since political conditions in the Middle East in 1983 were relatively stable, and the Camp David Accords, signed five years earlier, seemed to be holding. The biggest concern at the time was hyperinflation, which in Israel in the early 1980s was running at 500–1,000 percent per year, a level unimaginable to Americans. People would take paper currency, which was losing value daily, even hourly, and buy any commodity that maintained its value— eggs, furnishings, appliances, even toilet paper. Prices were not written on restaurant menus or food wrappers as they changed too quickly. Even the *Jerusalem Post,* the country's main English-language newspaper, did not print a price on its masthead.

During these hyperinflationary periods Israeli citizens went into "survival mode," spending the bulk of their time ensuring their families had a place to live, clothes to wear, and enough to eat. This was another reason why we had difficulty meeting locals—their minds were focused on the daily grind of living, not greeting short-term visitors from Minnesota. Since my Hebrew University salary was paid in *shekels,* the local unit of currency, I had to deal with the same problems faced by my neighbors. My wife and I spent a good deal of time turning our paper currency into hard goods. We learned to appreciate the financial health and stability too often taken for granted in the United States. Even the Savings and Loan crisis of the 1980s and the subprime mortgage and housing foreclosure woes of 2009–10 seem limited in impact compared with the ravages of hyperinflation that wreak financial havoc on every single resident without exception.

For most people, an overseas vacation opens one's eyes solely to the beauty and splendor of a holiday destination while glossing over the serious and debilitating problems faced by those living in the third world or a developing economy. This is the case when you lounge on the beach of Ocho Rios, Jamaica, ignorant of the poverty and ramshackle slums of Kingston. It is what happens when you limit your African visit to the wonders of the Masai Mara and Serengeti without dealing with the corruption and graft of daily Nairobi life, or when you experience the majestic mountain scenery of Nepal without learning about the Maoist revolt that devastated the countryside, or seeing the tragic consequences of forced child labor.

While there is nothing wrong with enjoying the unique sights of a country, one of the benefits of living overseas for a significant length of time is that both its beauty and ugliness, wonders and warts, impressive successes and dismal failures are revealed for you to think about, digest, and debate. Even if you and your family are not directly affected by these problems it is likely that neighbors, colleagues, and friends will be, and their worries and concerns will become part of your everyday conversations. The philosopher and theologian St. Augustine best captured this aspect of globetrotting when he wrote, "Tourists see the world, travelers experience it."

During our three months in Israel we had far fewer overseas visitors (due to the distance and a fear of terrorism, not my ability to say "No"), and we did not meet as many locals as in England, but this did not deter us from having a superb time. While locals are indispensable for exposing and understanding a country's soul, and visiting friends and relatives, in moderation, are an enjoyable diversion, the nuclear family is a fully satisfying "unit" for sightseeing and travel. We rented a car for three months and, on weekends and university holidays, used it to discover the Israel that lies outside Jerusalem. (Local buses were fine for getting around the city itself.)

We drove south to the Red Sea port of Eilat for great swimming and snorkeling. We motored north to Caesarea, Haifa, Sea of Galilee, the Golan Heights, all the way to Israel's northern border with Lebanon where a "thoughtful" guard let our 10-year-old daughter pose for a picture with his M-16 machine gun, minus ammo clip!

We drove to the Dead Sea, the lowest point on earth, and walked 1,300 feet to the top of Masada. (A horrible mistake in the heat of a July afternoon. Take the cable car!) Since the Camp David Accords had opened the Israel/Egypt border, my wife and children hopped

Our 10-year-old daughter Rebecca holding an M-16.

on a bus and headed off to Egypt to gaze at the Sphinx, Pyramids of Gaza, and the outstanding collection of Tutankhamen artifacts at the Museum of Egyptian Antiquities in Cairo. We spent two nights in a kibbutz trying to understand and appreciate this uniquely Israeli mode of collective living. We would often leave Jerusalem on Friday afternoon, since it shuts down completely for the Jewish Sabbath, and head to the more cosmopolitan and secular, some would say more fun, Tel Aviv, with its many restaurants, theaters, and beaches.

Best of all, we were drawn to the multitude of sacred sites that make this city holy to three great monotheistic religions—Judaism, Christianity, and Islam. With a population of only 750,000 the city is home to 1,200 synagogues, 150 churches, and 100 mosques. We visited the Western Wall, King David's Tomb, Mount of Olives, Golgotha, and the Dome of the Rock. We walked the Via Dolorosa and saw the thirteen Stations of the Cross, where Jesus spent the last hours before crucifixion. In America, a building dating to 1700 is old. In England, the definition of antiquity is pushed back to the tenth or eleventh century. Jerusalem has been an important world city since the tenth century BCE, three thousand years, when King Solomon built the first temple.

When we returned to Minneapolis on August 31, 1983, we had seen and experienced a fascinating country and had learned a great deal about overseas travel that would stand us in good stead on future trips. I learned that it was no longer necessary to sit back and wait for an overseas offer to fall into my lap. Every newspaper article, TV show, radio program, or professional interaction has the potential to turn into a working vacation. A magazine story about the construction of a new university in sub-Saharan Africa could, with the appropriate inquiries, lead to an invitation to work with local faculty teaching classes and designing curriculum. A TV feature about a new primary care clinic in Southeast Asia could be viewed as a clarion call to health professionals working in the area of tropical medicine, and that exchange teacher visiting your school from South America could become the source of a future reciprocal invitation to visit his or her home country. Whenever you read about or hear about an overseas opportunity that might be applicable to you, initiate a personal or e-mail conversation with the people involved to determine if there is any way for you and your family to take advantage of it.

Those three months in Israel taught me that my family and I could do quite well on our own, without requiring an extensive support system in the host country. Having a large circle of friends or family is wonderful, and having locals to help with housing, banking, and shopping can certainly be of great benefit. However, although useful they are not essential. Never let a lack of contacts or family ties stop you from planning and carrying out a working vacation. You will meet people and, at a minimum, have yourself, spouse, and children to fill your days with activities. This is exactly what happened to us in Israel. Instead of a social calendar filled with neighborly dinners and departmental parties as happened in London, we occupied ourselves with family travel and cultural immersion. Both types of working vacations can be thoroughly enjoyable and fully satisfying.

Finally, I learned that even in a country undergoing serious internal problems and stress, such as hyperinflation, these concerns could be viewed as learning opportunities, not impediments to travel. Experiencing these problems personally, as long as they do not threaten health or safety, can provide a better understanding of and appreciation for the financial, political, and cultural plights affecting much of the world.

After my wife and I had absorbed the many lessons learned from our most recent trip we came to realize that the potential set of working vacation destinations had widened greatly. England had opened up our eyes; Israel had opened up the world.

CHAPTER 4

Hakuna Matata

In 1983 Israel was not the comfortable, well-established, first-world country it is today with a higher per capita income than many European nations. Life there could be challenging, and many twenty-first century luxuries we expect and demand in the United States were unavailable. If we could enjoy a working vacation in a developing nation such as Israel, how might we fare in an even poorer, third-world location? That question intrigued us as Ruth and I had talked for years about the possibility of working in East Africa, not just for the game parks but also its natural beauty and unparalleled archeological history. After our first two overseas adventures, both of which were professionally, culturally, and financially successful, I was feeling a bit cocky about where we could work and what kind of living conditions we could handle.

Because of that (perhaps unfounded) confidence we decided our next adventure should take us to Kenya, but how could I pull that off? What was the chance of meeting a Kenyan computer science professor at my next professional meeting? Near zero. What was the probability of the *Chronicle of Higher Education* publishing an article about computer science teaching shortages in East Africa? Rather small. Instead of sitting back and waiting for the improbable to happen, I decided to try a new approach, an approach that turned out to be startlingly obvious, absurdly simple, and amazingly successful—the cold call. Yes, that irritating technique used by salesman, politicians, and scammers worldwide would now be put to use for a very different purpose.

In fall 1986, well before the appearance of the World Wide Web, I journeyed to the main library of the University of Minnesota to track down the e-mail address of Dr. Anthony (Tony) Rodrigues, Chair of the Institute for Computer Science at the University of Nairobi, one of the better Information Technology (IT) programs in East Africa. Now all you need to do is visit the Web site, www. uonbi.ac.ke/staff-directory/. The Web has truly speeded up the job of tracking down obscure information.

I composed a letter that said, in abbreviated form:

Dear Dr. Rodrigues,

I am a Professor of Computer Science at Macalester College in St. Paul, MN. I have a Ph.D. in computing and have been teaching at the college level for twelve years. I would enjoy coming to the University of Nairobi for three months, June to August 1987, to teach a course, give public talks on topics in computer science education, and help out in the department in whatever ways might be useful to you and your staff. My goal is to contribute to your educational program, experience daily life in Kenya, and become, however briefly, a part of the local community. Please respond if you are interested and we can discuss the details at greater length. I look forward to hearing from you and hope we will be able to work out a contractual agreement that is mutually acceptable.

G. Michael Schneider, Professor

I attached a résumé giving my educational background, teaching experience, professional references, and scholarly interests. I included syllabi of courses I would be willing to teach and abstracts of workshops and presentations I could offer to faculty and students.

The response did not bounce back quite as quickly as it had from his Israeli counterpart, but it was forthcoming within the month. Unknown to me, my letter had arrived at a propitious moment as the University of Nairobi was planning a major upgrade of its offerings in technical fields such as medicine, engineering, and computer science. They were excited to have me visit, and after a few e-mail exchanges we worked out an arrangement whereby I would present a series of talks, consult on issues of curriculum redesign, and teach one course during the winter quarter. Kenya is in the southern hemisphere, so my summer break falls in the middle of their academic year. Remember that when applying for a summer teaching job—it can come in handy!

In exchange for these services, the University of Nairobi would provide one round-trip air ticket, modest on-campus accommodations, and a small living allowance. These funds, along with my regular Macalester salary (I was on a twelve-month pay schedule) and rental income from our house, would allow us to almost break even for the entire trip—not bad for a three-month "working safari" for a family of four.

However, those plans changed dramatically when our two children, now sixteen and thirteen, informed us that under no circumstances would they join us in this venture. As I knew would happen eventually, they had reached the age where hanging out with friends, playing video games, and going to the mall were far more appealing summer pastimes than spending a long period of forced interaction with mom and dad on the other side of the globe. I tried convincing them of the wondrous sights they'd see. No dice. I switched to begging, cajoling, even bribery. Still no sale.

We were at an impasse that appeared to have only three possible solutions: I could drag them along unwillingly and spend three unpleasant months with dispirited, unhappy teenagers—not a pleasant thought. I could cancel the trip entirely, or I could leave them in the care of responsible adults while my wife and I went on our merry way.

My guess is most people would choose option two and cancel the trip, bemoaning their bad fortune while promising to try again in a few years when the kids go off to college. That option did not appeal to us since there was no guarantee this unique teaching offer would repeat itself four years hence—successful cold calls have a notoriously short shelf life. So we asked one more time and, when they refused yet again, met with the parents of their best friends whom we knew very well and trusted thoroughly.

These close friends agreed to serve as surrogate parents for three months, a move motivated not only by friendship, and our agreement to pay all our children's living expenses, but also enlightened self-interest. Their own children, often bored and cranky during the long, hot summer months, would have full-time, live-in companions. It worked out well for all parties although to this day our adult children, who now must dive into their own wallets to support a travel habit, lament this lost opportunity for an all-expense-paid three-month holiday in Africa. They still can't believe we listened to their non-stop whining and complaining and allowed them to remain behind.

Of course I would have preferred that our children join us on this zoological, anthropological, and cultural odyssey, just as you would certainly enjoy having your entire family travel with you. But when that is no longer an option, throwing away a once-in-a-lifetime travel opportunity may not be the winning strategy. I understand that most parents do not want to leave their almost-but-not-quite adult children behind while they wander the globe; this runs counter to the parental instinct buried deep within our breast. In our case, this mutually voluntary three-month separation worked out very well as each family member got exactly what he or she wanted from the summer hiatus.

Before throwing in the towel when children balk at joining you, consider option three, traveling without the kids, with family or trusted friends acting in *loco parentis,* or sending the kids to summer camp for the duration of your overseas stay. No one will think you're a bad parent, and everyone, parents and children alike, will have a wonderful time. Certainly you will enjoy it more than sitting home moping about what could have been.

Now it was dumb luck that I had blindly contacted a school about teaching computer science just as they decided to improve that area of their curriculum. But good fortune is the handmaiden of perseverance and resolve—much like the joke about Joe praying to win the lottery. In frustration God responds "Joe, at least give me a chance—buy a ticket!" The likelihood of such a fortuitous coincidence is small, but if you don't even bother to contact a school and ask, the chances drop to zero.

Over the past three decades my unsolicited cold calls have been successful in obtaining postings in Kenya, Turkey, and Zimbabwe, experiences described in this and the following chapters. They were unsuccessful in my initial attempts to obtain positions in Bhutan and Palau, failures analyzed in detail in Chapter 7. However, even if your success rate is less than mine, a well-crafted query letter or blind e-mail has a surprisingly decent chance of producing a positive outcome. While skeptics will no doubt laugh at the idea of cold calling as a viable way of locating working vacations let me show you they are wrong, not just by saying it but by proving it mathematically!

Assume there is only one chance in twenty (probability $p = 0.05$) of success, i.e., of getting a "Yes, we really want you" response to your cold call or blind email. That means you will get back a "No thank you" nineteen times out of 20 ($p = 0.95$). Furthermore, let's say you contact four institutions, A, B, C, and D, trying to obtain that one dream offer. The likelihood that exactly one of these four places says Yes is equal to the chance of getting exactly one Yes and exactly three Nos, which is $(0.05) \times (0.95) \times (0.95) \times (0.95) = 0.0429$. However, that single Yes could come from either A, B, C, or D, so the overall probability of getting exactly one Yes from any one of your four inquiries is four times that previous number, or $4 \times 0.0429 = 0.1716$. (Please bear with me. I promise there won't be much more mathematics!)

However, the true odds are better than that. If you are a lucky individual you might get two Yeses in response to your four cold calls. Of course you cannot accept two jobs at the same time, but you are free to pick the one that best suits you. There are six different ways that two places can both say Yes: (A, B), (A, C), (A, D), (B, C), (B, D), and (C, D). The chance of any one of these events happening is the probability of getting exactly two Yeses and exactly two Nos, which is $(0.05) \times (0.05) \times (0.95) \times (0.95) = 0.0023$. So, the overall probability of getting exactly two Yeses from anywhere is $6 \times 0.0023 = 0.0138$. I won't go through the mathematics of exactly three and four Yeses (rare events) but the sum of all these values is the probability that you will receive at least one positive response to your four inquiries. That final total is 0.1855, or about 18.6%.

Now think about what that means. Even if you have only one chance in twenty of anyone being interested, simply by contacting four schools you have improved your chances of landing a position from one in twenty to 18.6%, almost one in five. If I told you that spending a little bit of time on your computer would result in a one in five chance of an all-expenses paid three-month safari to Kenya would you do it? Of course you would. Well, then, why haven't you!

Using the Web, it takes just a few seconds to obtain the name and address of a dean, director, or department head at virtually any school, clinic, government agency, or research center in the world.

Sending an e-mail describing your skills and inquiring about a short-term, temporary position takes virtually no time and costs nothing. So don't be afraid to try, and try as often as you like.[3]

For the third time in seven years we made our way to the international airport in Minneapolis and on May 22, 1987, flew to Nairobi, Kenya. Tony Rodrigues met us at the airport and was a marvelous host. We quickly discovered that he saw it as his duty, much like Morris at Imperial College, to ensure that we had a fascinating experience in his adopted country—Tony is from Goa, India, and had taught at Makerere University in Uganda. In 1972 Idi Amin exiled him from the country along with eighty thousand other citizens of Asian heritage.

Tony drove us to our apartment in the married student housing complex where we discovered that when he said the school would provide *modest* accommodations he was greatly overstating the situation. The place was a dreary, featureless apartment with little furniture, empty walls, sagging mattresses, and bare light bulbs dangling from the ceiling. Unlike other apartments in the neighborhood, though, it did have electricity, a functioning western toilet, a refrigerator, and a single counter-top cooking coil.

That night my vaunted cockiness and composure disappeared as I broke down and cried. I looked at our accommodations and was sure that this time I had overreached. Living here for three months would certainly test my equanimity and self-assurance. Once more nagging doubts and fears crept into my mind, and I wondered if this was all a colossal mistake. My wife had to literally wrap her arms around me and assure me that everything would work out for the best—much like a mother comforting a distraught child. Once more she was right as Kenya turned out to

---

3. Even if the odds of receiving a Yes are a dismal 50–1, sending out 8 e-mails will give you a 15% chance of landing a position; send out 15 and the odds go up to one in four–a heck of a lot better than the lottery!

be the most extraordinary and enriching travel experience of our still short traveling lives, bare light bulbs and all.

Because of our relative newness to the working-vacation concept we had not considered the obvious alternative to the problem of less than ideal housing. If the accommodations provided by your school or company are not to your liking then simply thank your hosts for what they have done, find a realtor, and make your own living arrangements realizing, of course, this will add significantly to your travel costs. In Kenya we chose to stay put. Years later, on a working vacation at the University of New South Wales in Sydney, Australia, the prearranged accommodations consisted of a tiny and rather depressing apartment in a married student dormitory. Since our financial situation at the time was far better than it had been in 1987, we opted to move out of the dorm and rent a lovely apartment in the elegant Rose Bay neighborhood of the city. When faced with the dilemma of substandard housing you must decide for yourselves which is more important—more money in your pocket or better living space.

The following morning Tony picked us up and took us to the Thorn Tree Cafe for breakfast, a famous outdoor bistro that was a gathering place for adventurers, big game hunters, guides, backpackers, and other assorted soldiers-of-fortune. Today it is simply a popular photo stop on the tourist bus route, but this was 1987 and it was people watching of the highest quality. After breakfast Tony helped me move into my office at the Institute and introduced us to Chris and Chegge, two young graduate students also teaching classes. They would become dear friends and join us on some of our remote bush trips. The fears and doubts of the previous night were already beginning to evaporate.

The next day we wandered the neighborhood and made a pleasant discovery—a local YMCA with an outdoor swimming pool surrounded by shaded chaise lounges, a perfect retreat for a warm, sunny afternoon. Even more surprising was what we encountered not two blocks from home: a traffic circle, dubbed by locals the "religious roundabout," rimmed by Catholic and Protestant churches as well as the Nairobi Hebrew Congregation. Yes, here in East Africa was a 105-year-old congregation serving the 175 Jewish families in the Nairobi area. We attended services the following Friday night and joined dozens of exuberant worshippers, black and white, in a service that could just have easily been in Minneapolis, Chicago, or Tel Aviv.

We returned to the synagogue whenever we were in town on a Friday night or Saturday morning, and could only marvel at how much our understanding of Jewish identity and culture was being remade. Prior to this trip I had assumed that my co-religionists resided exclusively in the United States, Israel, Russia, and Western Europe. Our discovery of thriving Jewish communities in London and Jerusalem came as no surprise, but the idea of a congregation in Kenya might have been seen as the start of a joke by some borscht-belt comedian. Our stay in Nairobi opened my eyes to the existence of Jewish *Diaspora*, Jewish communities outside Israel, throughout the world, an experience repeated a few years later when we lived in Harare, Zimbabwe, and had a choice of joining one of the *five* functioning synagogues in the city. Living overseas opens your eyes to the fascinating and sometimes totally unexpected aspects of our global society.

Later that afternoon we walked downtown, a short fifteen-minute stroll from our apartment, and passed the historic Norfolk Hotel. Its outdoor patio, the hundred-year-old Lord Delamere Terrace and Bar, is surrounded by lush tropical gardens and, even today, is one of the city's most popular watering holes and a traditional meeting point for safaris and big-game hunts. We meandered through the city's teeming outdoor fruit and vegetable markets and inspected the handmade wares of the many sidewalk hawkers. It was from them I learned my first two words of Swahili—*hakuna matata,* rough translation, "No problem." If they didn't have my size, *hakuna matata*; don't carry that color or that pattern, *hakuna matata*. A fuller, and perhaps better, translation might be, "Hey man, life is too short to worry about that."

We had dinner at a local African restaurant and ordered two local favorites, *nyama choma,* barbecued curried meat, and *ugali,* cornmeal porridge similar to polenta or grits. They were both delicious, the Kenyan equivalent of steak and french fries. We were astonished at the stark contrasts of this modern, yet third-world city with skyscrapers next door to mud huts, and million dollar homes cheek-to-jowl with unimaginably poor slums. When we returned to the apartment, filled with the sights and smells of our first two days in Nairobi, the empty walls, minimal furnishings, and paltry cooking facilities had long been forgotten. Instead of whining and grumbling, we poured out our thoughts about what we had seen in such a short time and began planning our activities for the coming week, the last one before school started and ate into our free time. A mere forty-eight hours had changed this simpering, nervous newbie into someone excited and eager to experience what the region had to offer. Fortunately, my wife is not of the "I told you so" school of debate.

The lesson to be learned from these first two days in Kenya is that if you are considering a working vacation open up your mind, as well as your atlas, to not only the obvious tourist destinations of Western Europe, Canada, Japan, Australia, and the like, but also to the less well-off but still safe and stable countries of Africa, South America, South Asia, Southeast Asia, and Micronesia. Even though living accommodations may sometimes be less opulent and the infrastructure a little less developed, any minor discomforts you experience will almost certainly disappear after your first encounters with the natural beauty of the area and the warmth and friendliness of the people. There will be no doubt in your mind what should be foremost when traveling—comfortable living conditions or becoming an integral part of a unique and fascinating non-Western culture. The former is a nice plus, but the latter is a truly transformative experience.

Our rental car was delivered the following day—a ten-year-old Nissan with bald tires and a ghastly brown and yellow two-tone paint job. But, looks aside, it was our ticket to explore the city and the Kenyan countryside. Our first excursion was to Olorgesailie Prehistoric Park, an archeological reserve built around a million-year-old Paleolithic dig excavated by Drs. Louis and Mary Leakey in the 1940s.

When we told people we were coming to Kenya one word sprang to everyone's mind, *safari,* a packaged tour consisting of an almost endless series of game-park excursions. These trips miss out on a unique opportunity—learning firsthand about the evolution of

Lone giraffe along the road to Olorgesailie Prehistoric Park. Our first animal sighting.

Homo erectus, the ancestor of modern man, in the Rift Valley area of Eastern Africa. Given three months to explore the country, we were not about to make this mistake. We piled into our car, hoping the engine was in better shape than the tires and body, and drove forty miles over the Ngong hills, *sans* map I might add, deep into the Rift Valley, with its spectacular African scenery. Along the way we had our "welcome to Africa" moment—a lone giraffe standing by the side of the highway serenely munching acacia leaves. To the local Kikuyu or Luo farmers that sight is probably as common as a squirrel collecting acorns is to a Midwesterner, but to us it was worth an extended stop and at least a dozen photos, the first of hundreds (thousands?) snapped during our stay.

When you live in a city like London, New York, or Tokyo, blessed with a superb urban transit system, you can easily get by without a car, renting one as needed for the occasional out-of-town trip. In Nairobi, with its unreliable, not to mention overcrowded and unsafe bus system, and many sights located far outside the city, you really need to rent a car for the duration of your stay. This can be an expensive undertaking, perhaps the largest cash outlay of the entire trip. Added to the expense of the rental are the high cost of gas and the likelihood of frequent repairs caused by poor roads, substandard replacement parts, and bad drivers. That being said, my advice is to "suck it up" and do it for the freedom it provides to explore the countryside and take advantage of the many adventures and cultural opportunities that will come your way.

During our three-month stay we participated in a traditional African wedding in the city of Machakos, about thirty miles east of Nairobi; visited the extended family of one of my students in a small Kikuyu village; and traveled with Chris and Chegge to pristine beaches on the Indian Ocean coast utterly unknown to tourists but popular with locals. None of these experiences would have been possible without access to a car.

To help keep costs down, I recommend not renting from a major international car rental company such as Hertz, Avis, or Budget. They are oriented toward daily and/or weekly rates that, when scaled to a two- or three-month contract (or longer) without some type of "volume discount," will certainly break the bank. For example, at a rate of $80/day, a three-month rental would total $7,000, a bit more than most of us are willing to shell out. Buying a car and re-selling it at the end of your stay is often not an option, as you will not have the papers and legal documents required for such a financial transaction.

A better choice is to negotiate a private rental. In many countries private citizens rent their personal cars to earn extra money, perhaps generating more income from this transaction than from their regular job. I rented my tired old Nissan from the friend of the mother of a Kenyan student attending Macalester. I contacted the mother prior to my arrival and let her know that I was in the market for a car for three months. She asked around and located someone willing to rent their car for $300 per month, double the average monthly salary of a Nairobi employee, but only a fraction of the rate charged by local agencies. I also had to purchase temporary automobile insurance from a local agent, as my regular policy did not include coverage when driving outside the United States, something you definitely want to check before leaving home. Even including the cost of this temporary policy, the overall cash outlay was far less than what it would have been for a commercial rental.

A similar incident occurred when we were living in Mauritius and rented from the cousin of a teaching colleague. He had been arrested for drunk driving and lost his driving privileges for one year; his legal entanglement became our good fortune. We rented his car for six months, while he ended up making a tidy profit from his mishap.

Before leaving on your trip, put out the word to anyone who might be of help in locating a private rental—colleagues and administrators at the host school or research center, employees of the U.S. Embassy, and parents and relatives of international students at your school. Such "shots in the dark" often pay off in unexpected and profitable ways.

Finally, if none of these approaches yield positive results consider advertising for a private rental in a local newspaper or check the Yellow Pages for car *leasing,* not rental, companies that may have more attractive, although still pricey, rates for long-term rentals. In any case, just remember that you are the recipient of a three- (or six- or nine-) month African holiday for a fraction the cost charged by upscale companies such as National Geographic or Abercrombie & Kent, where a luxury safari for two can run upwards of $15,000. So, get a car and enjoy the freedom and mobility it gives you without fretting over the cost.

After our successful navigation of the Rift Valley on unnumbered, unsignposted, and often unpaved Kenyan roads, my wife and I gained enough confidence to drive to even more distant sights, including many famous Kenyan game parks. We drove fifty miles to Lake Naivasha, a fresh water lake filled with hippos and home to over four hundred species of birds. We traveled another twenty miles to Lake Nakuru, famous for its huge flocks of flamingos. Along the way we encountered a most unusual traffic impediment, a two-ton cape buffalo as large as my Nissan that had decided to lie down and relax in the middle of the road. We parked and waited patiently until it moved on, hoping the massive beast did not get a sudden case of road rage!

We toured Nairobi National Park, so close to the city that the gleaming office buildings and hotel towers of downtown are visible on the horizon while you drive through virgin savannah enjoying the sight of free-roaming gazelle, wildebeest, zebra, and lion. It was here that we had our first of many minor breakdowns—a flat tire. Not a problem until you remember you are in an open, unprotected area filled with wild animals. My wife climbed on the bumper of the car, scanned the area with binoculars, and kept a close lookout for lions while I changed the tire—front doors ajar should we need to beat a hasty retreat.

Some game parks were either too far to reach by car or the roads were passable only by four-wheel drive vehicles. To visit these sites we needed to book a tour and it was then we discovered yet another benefit of a working vacation—the ability to purchase inexpensive tours from local travel agents at a fraction the cost of what you might expect to pay overseas. Packaged African tours purchased in the United States or Europe are oriented around assembling a complete, five-star, two- or three-week safari—air, van, hotel, meals, guides. These are frightfully expensive and not at all what you want or need when living in country. Instead, it is easy to go to a local travel agent and purchase, in the local currency, a stand-alone two- or three-day excursion, travel and accommodations included, at a reasonable cost.

My wife and I strolled downtown and purchased a three-day tour of the Masai Mara, traveling there in a small, single-engine plane; as well as a four-day trip to Arusha National Park and Ngorongoro Crater in Tanzania, where we drove to the border, parked our car in a long-term lot, walked through customs, and were picked up on the other side by a Tanzanian travel company van. Both of these exotic, once-in-a-lifetime trips were very professional and, best of all, highly affordable. It is almost always the case, especially in developing countries, that you should wait until you arrive to purchase local and regional tours, especially last-minute trips with unsold seats that may need to be moved quickly. You will be pleasantly surprised at how reasonable they can be.

The single most frequently asked question from friends and family is "Of all your travels what is the one place you loved the most?" My stock answer is that I've enjoyed them all—exactly the cop-out you get from any parent asked which of their children they love the most. However, if you were to insist that I not weasel out of answering, my response would have to be Ngorongoro Crater National Park in Tanzania. This is a hundred-square-mile sunken volcanic caldera encircled by mountains rising two thousand feet above the valley floor. The crater is filled with more than twenty-five thousand animals of virtually every species, including the big five—rhino, lion, elephant, leopard, and buffalo. As you drive into the crater via a dirt track dropping down at a stomach-wrenching 17 percent incline, the feeling you get is reminiscent of the undiscovered plateau in the 1912 book *The Lost World,* by Sir Arthur Conan Doyle. In this case, however, it is not a plateau keeping the animals in but a half-mile high mountain range.

That four-day Tanzanian safari was an unforgettable experience, especially as it was not a long-planned, carefully researched expedition but, instead, a spontaneous, "let's get out of town" jaunt, much as you might head to the Jersey shore on a summer weekend. Rather than pre-planning and pre-booking your entire holiday, which can be difficult in an unfamiliar country, a working vacation gives you the time to settle in, talk to locals, learn about those special out-of-the-way places you really must see, and book them from a local travel agent at your convenience and at a fraction of the cost. The result is your holiday becomes much more like life back home where you may read about an event or see a travel deal advertised in the newspaper and, on a whim, give it a try.

An event of a very different type occurred midway through our stay, and it is something that has stayed with my wife and me as much as, if not more than, any archeological dig, giraffe sighting, or African sunset. A neighbor gave us the name of her parish priest, Father George, who recently left his pulpit in Minnesota to work with the Missionaries of Charity in Nairobi, a worldwide organization established in Calcutta by the Nobel Peace Prize winner Mother Teresa. Its volunteers, both lay and clergy, are committed to helping the neediest members of society—lepers, AIDS sufferers, prostitutes, orphans, the abused, abandoned, and disfigured. Following our arrival we contacted Father George, who invited us to join him as he made his rounds of Kibera, a place utterly unimaginable to anyone who has not traveled outside the first world.

Kibera is the largest slum in the Nairobi area and the second largest in Africa, after Soweto in Johannesburg. It covers only one square mile but is home to eight hundred thousand people, with some estimates topping a million. This produces a population density of three hundred thousand people/km², ten times greater than that of Mumbai, India, the most densely populated city in the world. Dilapidated dwellings rise atop mounds of rotting garbage and human waste, and due to steep terrain and the complete absence of sewers and drains these deteriorated residences often flood during the rainy season. Although the Kibera neighborhood is geographically within the city of Nairobi, it is not really part of it as the police routinely refuse to enter, and it has no access to basic city services such as water, sanitation, and electricity.

We spent the day in Kibera with Father George, distributing food and medical supplies, participating in last rites for the dying, drinking tea, and talking with residents. It was a disturbing but highly enlightening experience. Unlike many slums in the United States, the dominant emotions in Kibera are not anger and rage but determination and persistence. Residents go to Herculean efforts—for example, walking two hours each way to menial jobs in the central city—to improve their lot and provide for their children. Hearing their stories made me embarrassed by my initial reaction to our apartment with its lumpy mattresses and bare light bulbs. It also made my wife and me mindful of why these working vacations were becoming such an important part of our lives.

One word of caution, though. Our visit was by invitation of someone living and working in Kibera. He wanted us to experience, firsthand, conditions in the slums, bring that knowledge back to the United States, and share it with students and colleagues at Macalester, which I did. In 1987 my wife and I were among only a tiny handful of Western visitors to spend any time in those squalid streets. The situation today is completely different because of a new form of niche travel called "poverty tourism" available from agencies, large and small, around the world. These companies provide comfortable, safe, and fully narrated bus tours of not only Kibera but the slums of Calcutta, townships of South Africa, shantytowns of Mexico City, and *favelas* of Rio de Janeiro. In the last few years slum visits have become a fashionable form of day tripping, as world-weary travelers grow bored of the standard menu of museums, shopping, and beaches.

Proponents of the tours cite the educational experience of learning about living conditions in the slums. They argue they are providing desperately needed jobs for bus drivers and tour guides as well as creating valuable opportunities for residents to sell locally made handicrafts to visitors. They also believe the embarrassment of tourists witnessing horrific living conditions just a few miles from their own five-star luxury accommodations will put pressure on local politicians to clean up and improve these neighborhoods. Opponents argue this is simply a way for unscrupulous travel agents to make money off the humiliation and poverty of others, and there is precious little education to be gained snapping photos of shantytowns from a bus window. An editorial in the *Daily Nation,* Kenya's largest newspaper, castigated movie stars, well-heeled businessmen, and other dignitaries for their fascination with slums like Kibera, perhaps fueled by the popularity of the 2005 movie *The Constant Gardener* in which it played a starring role.

It is quite possible that future working vacations will take you and your family to some of the poorest nations in the world, much like this trip to Kenya as well as our later visits to Nepal and Mongolia. Poverty tourism is a moral issue you need to think about and resolve in your mind as you mull over proffered visits to urban slums, charity hospitals, leper colonies, and other places of poverty, pain, and despair. Of course there is no universal answer to this dilemma, and you will need to decide each case individually based on the goals of the visit, the benefits it brings to residents, and whether you and your family will learn and grow from this highly emotional experience.

About a month before our departure we had our first and only visitor from the United States, my sister Karen who came for a two-week stay. Ruth and I drove to the airport, accompanied by Tony who insisted on joining us to ensure we got there safely. I tried to convince him that if I could navigate the three hundred miles from Nairobi to Mombassa, a trip successfully completed just one week earlier, I could certainly handle the thirteen miles to the airport and back. He remained unconvinced and plopped down in our back seat. On the return to our apartment we could already sense "sparks" flying between the two of them, both single and about the same age. Two days later Tony informed us that he and Karen were flying to Zanzibar for a beach holiday and would return ten days later, only one day before her scheduled return to the United States. So much for that visit. We never even got a postcard.

Karen returned to Africa the following year, where Tony proposed marriage. However, he was adamant that he would not leave his home and his work in Kenya, so if she accepted she would have to move to Nairobi from her condo in Del Mar, California—a relocation of staggering proportions. After long and agonizing deliberations she decided she could not bring herself to become a Kenyan, said no, and returned to the United States. Too bad; I was looking forward to some unique family get-togethers on the plains of the Serengeti.

As with our two earlier working vacations, this one ended well before we were ready to leave. On our final day in Nairobi my feelings of satisfaction and delight were in marked contrast to the gnawing doubts and fears experienced that first day. We had made many close friends with whom we have remained in contact. We traveled the country and saw sights both expected (animals, game parks, archeology) and totally unexpected (an African wedding, the Nairobi Jewish community, the slums of Kibera). Best of all in those three short months we learned a great deal about life in Kenya and began to feel like residents of the community.

When we returned to Minneapolis in early September 1987, my wife and I agreed that this Kenyan adventure had cemented our dedication to long-term travel and convinced us that living and working overseas would be a permanent part of our professional lives. The working holidays described in the last three chapters—England, Israel, and Kenya—had brought us to the point where were no longer newbies. Instead, we were well on our way to gaining a reputation as seasoned, street-savvy world travelers able to adapt to and flourish in different cultures, a reputation those around us were beginning to notice. Family members, friends, and colleagues started inquiring how I was able to locate, plan, and finance these exotic vacations. More and more I found myself relating travel stories and sharing ideas about how they could create these work experiences for themselves. Thus began my lifelong passion for storytelling and helping others live and work overseas.

Ruth and I did not promise we would duplicate this working vacation experience every X years, as we were quite aware that our future travel schedule would depend on funding, work, family, health, and job availability. However, we did commit to doing everything in our power to locate and take advantage of whatever overseas opportunities might arise in the future. We also pledged ourselves to ensuring that X would never become too large.

CHAPTER 5

The City That Never Sleeps

I subscribe to the Woody Hayes school of logic. Hayes, a legendary football coach for twenty-eight years at Ohio State University, started every game by sending his strongest running back into the middle of the line. If the opponents stopped him for little or no gain, he would try something different. If, however, they could not slow down or impede his forward progress, Hayes would run the same play over and over again until they proved they could. His reasoning was eminently logical—why change a winning strategy?

My cold call to Tony Rodrigues at the University of Nairobi resulted in a hugely successful, once-in-a-lifetime East African experience. So, as Woody would say, why change? In early 1991, a little more than three years after returning from Kenya, Ruth and I were once again suffering the initial pangs of travel withdrawal, so we sat down and asked ourselves where in the world we might like to go. It was my wife who suggested Istanbul, Turkey, a destination she had dreamed about visiting for many years. Thank God she had not seen the 1978 movie *Midnight Express* describing the experiences of a young American tourist thrown into a nightmarish Turkish jail for drug smuggling. The movie single-handedly killed Turkish tourism for years.

I decided to try the cold call approach once again and send an out-of-the-blue e-mail to colleges and universities in Istanbul asking if they might be interested in hosting a summer computer science visitor from the United States. This time, however, there was a new wrinkle added to my job hunting. I was proposing to visit a country where English is neither an official language, as in England and Kenya, nor a semi-official language, as in Israel. It is Turkish, utterly unknown to me, that is the language of instruction at all educational levels. I could no more assume to walk into class and begin teaching in English than a Ph.D. from China could arrive at Macalester and start lecturing in Mandarin.

With this in mind, I visited the school library to do a little research on Turkish universities (although e-mail had become widely available the World Wide Web was still a year or two away) and found, to my great surprise, that the catalog for Bogazici University, the premier technical university in Turkey—essentially, their MIT—clearly stated on page one:

> The medium of instruction at Bogazici University is English. Applicants must have a TOEFL (Test of English as a Foreign Language) score of 550 or they need to sign up for an English language proficiency class.

Yet another "flashbulbs and trumpets" moment—that one paragraph had immediately eliminated the first of my two big hurdles. I now knew where I would be applying, but I still needed to generate a job offer.

One of the unexpected but pleasant surprises encountered during my overseas job hunting is how rapidly English is becoming the universal medium of instruction for tertiary instruction, even in countries where it is not an official language. This is particularly true in technical fields such as the physical sciences, natural sciences, engineering, and medicine, but it is also becoming widespread in other quantitative fields such as management, finance, architecture, pharmacy, public policy, and urban planning. In addition to Turkey I have lectured in English in Mongolia, Nepal, Japan, and Vietnam—none of which have English as one of their official national languages.

In Malaysia I attended a graduation address by then Prime Minister Dr. Mahathir bin Mohamad on the role of English as the *lingua franca* of science and international business, and the need for all Malaysians to become bilingual with proficiency in both Bahasa Malaysia and English. Apparently many people are getting the message, not just Malaysians. On the drive to the Ngorongoro Crater in Tanzania described in the previous chapter, I filled the car with gas at a remote Rift Valley station, the only one for miles and a popular rest stop for tour buses. Knowing this would be a good sales location, a young Masai warrior in a flowing red robe set up his souvenir table next to the pump. I was interested in buying a spear so I dug out my phrase book and uttered in grammatically butchered Swahili, *"Nini gharama mkuki?"* meaning "What price spear?" He smiled and replied in perfect New Yorkese, "No sweat, man. I speak English!"

I don't share these stories because of any Anglophone chauvinism or deep devotion to my mother tongue. It is simply to convince you not to immediately abandon hope for that dream teaching position in Surinam, Sarawak, or Senegal because of any perceived language inadequacy. In fact, English speaking and writing skills may actually work in your favor as overseas colleges and universities are often looking to hire native English speakers to improve their students' proficiency in the language. In addition, if your spouse has ESL teaching credentials, he or she should be able to find a teaching or private tutoring position using those skills, and might even wind up being more in demand than you!

As it turns out the second hurdle—a job offer—was also not a problem. I received an e-mail offer of employment from Prof. Selahattin Kuru, the chair of Computer Science at Bogazici University, within two weeks of my initial inquiry. In his response he proposed that I teach one ten-week summer school class and give some technical talks to students and faculty in exchange for a single round-trip air ticket from Minneapolis to Istanbul, on-campus housing for my wife and me, and a modest cash allowance. Modest, I might add, in terms of purchasing power, not in terms of absolute amount. My wife and I were to become "Turkish millionaires," receiving a monthly stipend of 1,200,000 Turkish *liras,* the local unit of currency. Unfortunately, with *lira* then trading at 2,400 to the dollar, that two-inch thick wad of bills I collected and stuffed into my pockets each month amounted to only $500.

By this fourth overseas working vacation I was coming to understand that these terms—one round-trip air ticket, on-campus housing, and a small food and living allowance—were pretty much the norm and roughly what you might expect to receive on your own working vacation. These funds, along with my regular monthly Macalester paycheck and the rental income from our home, were usually adequate to cover expenses. If you work at a college or university that allows you to spread out your nine- or ten-month academic salary over a twelve-month period, I strongly encourage you to do so. It makes budgeting for a summer working vacation much easier.

One of the realities of negotiating an offer with an overseas institution is that there may be little or no "wiggle room" regarding the financial terms. Faculty pay scales are often set by the university administration or central government, not the dean or department head, leaving little room to maneuver. However, while salaries may be somewhat inflexible there may be room for negotiations with regard to workload. Don't be surprised if your host institution initially proposes a heavy course load, dozens of public lectures, or consulting with a multitude of groups, since the director, department chair, or dean will naturally want to squeeze as much valuable work out of your visit as possible. The same applies to other disciplines.

A doctor may be asked to see hundreds of patients; the engineer may be assigned a six- or six-and-a half-day work week; the consultant may be asked to meet with dozens of agencies. Don't be afraid to respond that this is too great a workload for you to be able to do a quality job, and it needs to be lowered to a more manageable level. Then discuss a compromise workload acceptable to you and the host institution. You may not be able to negotiate the amount they are paying you, but you should be able to negotiate the amount of work you must do to earn that pay.

I e-mailed the chair that his terms were acceptable, set the date for our arrival, and began planning our Turkish working holiday. Rather than fly to Istanbul via Amsterdam or London, as they had proposed, I asked the school to purchase a ticket departing one week earlier and routed via Athens. As this did not increase their cost they were happy to do so—a bit surprising given the historical animosity between Greeks and Turks. Then, for a modest fee, after receiving our tickets in the mail we changed the itinerary, extending our layover in Athens from four hours to seven days!

A great way to turn your working vacation into an even more enjoyable holiday is to take that free ticket from A (your home) to B (your destination) and convert it into an "almost-free" ticket from A to C to B, where C is any destination along the way to B that you would enjoy visiting. Essentially, you are converting your free ticket into a "twofer" by adding a second stop. We spent a glorious week in Athens and the Greek islands before continuing on to Istanbul.

We repeated this gambit on subsequent working vacations to Zimbabwe (via Lisbon, Portugal; and Cape Town, South Africa),

Mauritius (via Mumbai, India), Australia (via the Fiji Islands) and Mongolia (via Beijing, China). In all cases the extra charge for extending our stay in the stopover city was small when compared with the cost of purchasing a full-fare ticket from Minneapolis to that same destination. When planning air travel to the host country, don't inquire only about direct flights, unless you are traveling with children when that may be the most important consideration. Instead, see what airlines fly to your ultimate destination, where they stop, and what the cost would be for extending your stay at a stopover city either on the way there or on the return. You might be pleasantly surprised at how little it costs (sometimes nothing) to add a few days in some attractive getaway to your already attractive working vacation.

After a week of seeing the historical sights of ancient Greece, eating in the Plaka neighborhood of Athens, and swimming in the blue-green waters of Paros and Mykonos, we returned to Athens and flew onward to Istanbul. My teaching assistant (TA), Mr. Albert Levy, picked us up at the airport. Yes, that is his real name. Albert is a fourth-generation Turkish Jew, and he was to be our entrée into the large, active Jewish community of Istanbul. The school did not assign him to me for that reason, and was as surprised as I was to find out that we were both Jewish.

We drove the fifty miles from the airport to the school in Albert's car as I sat back and took in the horizon-to-horizon sprawl of this massive city. As we drove, visions of that "modest" Nairobi apartment raced through my head, and I played guessing games about what our on-campus housing would look like. Bare light bulbs dangling from the ceiling? Maybe. Western toilet? Perhaps. Comfortable mattresses? Doubtful. Hot shower? No way. Reminding myself of the enjoyment we had on our East African getaway in spite of the less than plush accommodations, I decided I could make do with whatever the school might provide. Fortunately, my fears were unfounded. That summer we lived like an upper-middle class American couple, comfortably ensconced in a leafy, well-to-do suburban neighborhood.

Bogazici University, originally called Roberts College, was founded in Istanbul in 1863 by two American educators and philanthropists from New England. They purchased a large, wooded plot of land on a steep hill overlooking the Bosporus and set about creating a university where English was the medium of instruction, admission would be open to students of all races and religions (unusual at that time for a Muslim country), and the curriculum would be modeled on the American university system. In 1912, a wealthy donor gave the college money to build six elegant faculty homes, as the academic traditions of the time dictated that senior professors live on campus to be near their students. Since the school was founded by New Englanders, these six homes were built in classic Georgian colonial style, complete with chimneys, porticos, white wooden siding, and black shutters. These stately dwellings would not be out of place today in Boston, Hartford, or Providence, but they certainly look strange sitting in the middle of Istanbul on the border between Europe and Asia.

Today, these large, comfortable homes are no longer allocated to individual senior faculty but are used to house visitors coming to the university for short stays. Two, three, or even four families will often share a single house, depending on family size and length of stay. Since this was summer when there are far fewer visitors, we were its sole residents. We ended up living in a beautiful colonial home on five-plus acres of forested land in the middle of this densely packed urban area of sixteen million. The only comparison I can offer is to imagine living in an elegant and spacious New York City residence situated smack in the middle of Central Park.

Some of our Turkish visitors jokingly commented we were living as well as, perhaps slightly better than, the president of Turkey. While this was a bit of hyperbole, there is no doubt our housing that summer was superb and totally unexpected. When a school chooses to provide housing for you, rather than have you find it yourself, be aware that it can fall anywhere on the spectrum from minimally acceptable, as in Kenya, to off-the-scale luxurious, as was the case in Turkey. All you can do is hope for the latter but be willing to accept the former, or be willing to find and pay for your own accommodations.

Our time in Istanbul resulted in another busy and remarkable three-month sojourn. We made good friends among the computer science faculty as many had received their Ph.D.'s in the United States (Purdue University, University of Florida, Polytechnic University of Brooklyn) and were eager to renew professional as well as social contacts with American academics. We became good friends with Albert and the other twenty-something summer school TAs who would ask us to join them on their student-oriented weekend jaunts to bars, clubs, and concerts—making my wife and me feel quite old, I might add.

The days I was not teaching were filled with trips to major tourist sites such as Topkapi Palace, Hagia Sophia, and the Blue Mosque, as well as more leisurely activities such as riverboat excursions to the Black Sea, meetings with members of the Turkish Jewish community (courtesy of Albert), and a visit to the village of Kanlica on the Asian side of the Bosporus. According to my colleagues Kanlica is famous for making the world's richest, creamiest, and most delicious yogurt. After traveling there by water taxi and enjoying some at a local restaurant, we could only agree. This off-the-beaten path "yogurt outing" is typical of the unusual but thoroughly delightful activities in which you can participate when given adequate time. Kanlica would definitely not be on the itinerary of your typical four-day/three night "Highlights of Istanbul" packaged tour.

We also had time for weekend excursions to destinations farther afield, such as the three thousand-year-old archeological ruins of Ephesus, the volcanic rock formations and cave homes of

Capadocchia, and the beach resort of Bodrum. These tours were purchased from a local travel agent after our arrival and paid for in *lira,* making all three trips quite reasonable compared with their cost if purchased in the United States.

Many days we would not go into the central city but, instead, sit for hours on the outdoor terrace of the Bebek Hotel, close to campus and overlooking the Bosporus—Bogazici means Bosporus in Turkish. We would sip coffee (in the morning) or a glass of wine (in the evening) watching river traffic sail by and enjoying the sight of the setting sun illuminating the Asian side of the straits.

To learn about a country and its people most visitors, ourselves included, head off to museums, historical sites, churches, mosques, and parks. Food, however, is an important component of culture, in some countries one of the most important, and a cooking class can be an entrée into a totally different aspect of a region's history and traditions. Turkish food, although not as well-known to American palates as French, Italian, or Chinese, has influenced cooking styles and eating habits throughout the Mediterranean. My wife and I signed up for a one-day cooking class that included not only cooking instruction—and eating, of course—but also an introduction to local shopping habits and Middle Eastern mealtime rituals.

We bought groceries in the local *souk* (marketplace) under the tutelage of our instructor and then returned to her kitchen to make *mezes* (appetizers), *dolma* (stuffed grape leaves), *mercimek* (lentil soup), the ubiquitous *kebabs,* and the national dish of Turkey, *Hünkar Beğendi* (meaning literally, "The Sultan Loved It"), which is composed of lamb, eggplant, and *cashar* cheese. Our "classroom lessons" were consumed during a leisurely two-hour dinner washed down with many glasses of *raki,* a popular anise-flavored alcoholic drink. Check out www.cookingalaturka.com to read about one of the oldest and best-known Turkish cooking schools.

When thinking about how to best use the extended time available on a working vacation, consider not only the major tourist sites listed in Frommer's and the Lonely Planet, but also some less well-known introductions into the traditions, habits, and customs of your host country. This includes not only cooking classes, but courses on language, dress, music, dance, and traditional crafts; visits to people's homes; sporting events; involvement with a local religious community; volunteering at a neighborhood school; or assisting at a community center or senior citizen home. It is difficult to participate in these types of activities on a rigidly scheduled packaged tour, but they fit quite comfortably into a working-vacation regimen whose duration is a few months rather than a few days. Faculty colleagues and neighbors, as well as the Web, can be good sources of information and advice on how to locate and sign up for these classes, home visits, and volunteer opportunities.

It was in İstanbul where we had our first encounter with an issue we had totally overlooked during our first three working vacations—the cost of overseas health care. Ruth came down with a mild ear infection but one still serious enough to warrant a doctor's visit and a prescription for antibiotics. Fortunately the problem cleared up in a week or so, and my out-of-pocket expenses were small, but it was sufficiently unnerving for us to think seriously about purchasing international health insurance on all future working vacations, a concern that should have been on our minds from the very outset—perhaps we weren't yet as sophisticated and street-savvy as we had imagined.

On the second page of every United States passport the State Department prints the following stern warning:

> Medical costs abroad can be extremely expensive. Does your insurance apply overseas, including medical evacuation, payment to the overseas hospital or doctor, or reimbursement to you later?

You are then referred to their brochure, "Medical Information for Americans Abroad," available on-line at http://travel.state.gov/travel/tips/brochures/brochures_1215.html. It is an excellent document to read before starting any overseas adventure.

When planning a working vacation it is critical that you check with your local health-care provider to determine exactly what they will and will not cover while you are abroad, including any restrictions on injuries and illnesses, maximum length of stay, and exclusions for the country of residence. If you are one of the lucky few whose policy includes full international coverage, then no more need be done. (Note: Some international exchange programs, such as Fulbright grants, include health coverage in their benefits.) But the great majority of policies contain either significant overseas restrictions or come to a complete and crashing halt at our national borders. In these cases you need to consider supplemental health-care coverage for you and your family, and a good place to start your investigation is at the HTH Worldwide Web site http://www.hthtravelinsurance.com/. Then click on the link "Travel Medical and International Health Insurance Basics."

There are two types of international health policies: Travel Health Insurance pays for such basics as emergency medical needs, ambulance services, hospital costs, doctor bills, and prescription medicines. In the event of a serious injury or illness requiring specialized treatment, Emergency Evacuation Insurance covers the cost of evacuating you to your home in the United States or to the nearest full-service health center, a cost that can often run tens of thousands of dollars. You should consider purchasing both types of insurance to avoid a catastrophically large medical bill.

When comparing policies keep in mind the following three issues: 1) Duration. Some policies are capped at thirty, sixty, or ninety days at which point they immediately terminate. This doesn't do you any good if your working vacation extends beyond the termination date. Make sure the policy lasts at least as long as your appointment. 2) Primary/secondary coverage. A primary-care policy pays all medical expenses regardless of what other insurance you may have while a secondary policy covers only costs in excess of the amount you will be reimbursed from existing policies. Primary coverage is an unnecessary luxury if your current insurer will pay a portion of the expenses. Purchase a policy that covers only your actual out-of-pocket costs. 3) Deductibles and co-pays. Like most health policies, the more you are personally willing to pay the cheaper the cost will be. Determine how much you are willing to risk while overseas and then purchase a policy with the appropriate-size deductible.

The exact cost of a joint travel health/emergency evacuation health policy will vary greatly based on the factors mentioned above—duration, coverage type, and deductibles—as well as your age, family size, and host country. But, as just one example, the approximate cost of a policy providing travel health-care and emergency-evacuation coverage for a forty-something adult living and working in Istanbul, Turkey, is about $135 to $300 per month. This is not a lot to pay for a very important aspect of a working vacation—peace of mind!

While living in Turkey Ruth and I received e-mail from a Macalester colleague, a Classics professor who travels annually to Greece for teaching and research. This year he wanted to add a stopover in Turkey to view its many classical highlights—Ephesus, Troy, the Temple of Aphrodite—but he and his wife were somewhat hesitant, scared off by a misguided perception of Turkey as unclean, dangerous, even somewhat "sinister." (Perhaps they had seen *Midnight Express*.) When they learned that Ruth and I were living in Istanbul they asked if we might consider being their hosts and guides to the city, helping them avoid the problems experienced by naive travelers visiting a strange, new place. We were happy to accommodate them, and I arranged for someone to pick them up at the airport and made room reservations at a convenient hotel. For three busy days the four of us walked the old city, saw the sights, ate at local restaurants without anyone getting sick—one of their big worries—and went to some of my favorite clubs to listen to superb Middle Eastern music. Their fears soon dissipated, and my colleague realized how silly he had been to wait so long before visiting this magical, not sinister, city. (He has returned many times since.) Before departing he thanked us profusely for being such experienced travelers and making him feel so safe and relaxed in an unfamiliar place.

For us this was "official confirmation" that Ruth and I had completed the transformation from working-vacation newcomers to experienced, knowledgeable world travelers. Here was a Classics professor, whose very subject of study is the Eastern Mediterranean including Turkey, asking a computer scientist, of all people, for help in seeing the country and navigating its geographical, social, and cultural maze. From the "Nervous Nellie" in Chapter 2 who was frightened by the mere idea of moving to England, by the end of this fourth working vacation, eleven years later, I had gained the skill and confidence needed not only to live and work overseas but to guide others through the orientation needed to feel comfortable in a strange new culture.

As September 1, our departure date, approached we reflected upon how much Istanbul reminded us of New York City, not in terms of history, ethnicity, or architecture, but rather in terms of its scale, vibrancy, and the enjoyment of life and its many pleasures. It is a city that never sleeps. Two in the morning is prime time for thousands of people enjoying the Taksim music scene; the cars, taxis, and buses clogging streets; and the street vendors hawking *simit*, Turkish bagels, and *döner kebabs*, what Americans call *gyros*. It is a city where you can spend countless hours shopping, eating, sipping coffee, and strolling the hundreds of neighborhoods that sprawl over this massive urban area. During our three months in Istanbul we explored perhaps one-tenth of this fascinating city. I can't imagine how little you would be able to drink in given only one or two weeks. Cities like Istanbul, as well as London, Tokyo, New York, Paris, Shanghai (and others) demand time, lots of time, to come to understand and appreciate their immense historical and cultural riches. A working vacation gives you that time.

One year later, in early 1992, I decided to follow Woody Hayes's advice and make yet another cold call. So far nothing but sevens had appeared whenever I rolled the dice and sent out unsolicited letters. Could it happen once again?

CHAPTER 6

Back to Africa

There are two types of world travelers—the *repeaters* and *not agains*. Repeaters have found their one dream destination and go back year after year to the same village, the same B&B, even the same room. They are the couple who return every March, like swallows to Capistrano, to that quaint little inn in the south of France; who pre-book every year at their special hacienda on the Mayan Riviera; who canoe the same river and eat at the same restaurant, year in, year out. In contrast, the not agains love the places they have been but prefer to seek out new sights and unexpected adventures. Repeaters are the "bird in the hand" group, not agains the "two in the bush."

I have no quibble with repeaters and congratulate them on discovering their one perfect Eden. Even better, the task of locating the next working vacation is far simpler for repeaters than for the not agains. After completing that first visit, sit down with school, agency, or institute administrators, tell them how much you enjoyed your stay, and ask if they would be interested in hosting a return visit in the near future. Assuming you have not screwed up too badly and funds are available, there is a decent chance they will be eager to have you come back, and the planning for your next working vacation will have been accomplished. Nice and simple. I followed that path myself after a 2007 cold call resulted in a six-month visiting professorship at Columbia University in New York City, home of my now-grown children and grandchildren. I re-negotiated that initial offer into a return visit for the 2008–09 academic year and beyond, at my discretion.

However, in 1992 my wife and I belonged to the latter group, the not agains. We loved our first four working vacations and found each city—London, Jerusalem, Nairobi, Istanbul—a destination not plumbed to its fullest depths. Each site still tempted with possibilities of fresh explorations and new discoveries. When we would return home, bubbling with stories about the sights we'd seen and the people we'd met, friends and family were sure that our next trip would take us back to the same place—working vacation redux. In three decades of travel, until our return to New York City and Columbia, it never has. As much as we've enjoyed and savored each and every trip, when it came time to think about and plan the next one we would stare at a world map and see too much unexplored space, too many countries not stabbed with a pushpin. The United Nations has 192 member states and so far we had lived and worked in 4 outside the U.S. It seemed much too early for reruns.

Our Kenyan friends and colleagues said that if we enjoyed our time in East Africa we should really consider a trip to Zimbabwe, the country called Rhodesia until 1980 when it won its independence from Great Britain in a bloody civil war. After reading about its rich culture, natural beauty, and superb historical sites, Ruth and I decided that a working vacation to Zimbabwe would be an excellent way to relive the delights of our Kenyan safari, now seven years distant, but with different places to explore and new people to meet.

At that time Zimbabwe was the success story of sub-Saharan Africa, and its capital, Harare, was one of the loveliest cities on the continent. This is hard to fathom given conditions there today—famine, cholera, hyperinflation, and civil unrest—all thanks to a once-benevolent president, Robert Mugabe, who devolved into a brutal dictator with a death grip on power and an intolerance of public dissent.[4]

In 1992 things were quite different and Harare was a charming city of pedestrian malls, upscale shopping, and outdoor cafes, all frequented by a large, thriving black middle class. With its broad downtown avenues shaded by jacaranda trees and lined with busy stores, it would have been hard for most Americans to believe they were in Africa. It was a city that, at least in 1992, would shatter the stereotype that all of sub-Saharan Africa looks like a Sally Struthers public service announcement for "Save the Children."

The University of Zimbabwe, called UZ by locals, sits in the leafy middle class suburb of Mt. Pleasant, about four miles north of downtown. It was founded in 1952 in cooperation with the University of London, and until the recent troubles was one of the finest schools in southern Africa. It was certainly the place where I would prefer to teach. To that end I followed the same sequence of operations successful twice before—using the local library to learn the name and address of the chair of the Computer Science Department and then sending e-mail inquiring about summer teaching, being sure to include a résumé, references, syllabi of courses I could teach, and abstracts of public lectures I could deliver. Bingo! Not two weeks later I received a positive response

---

4. Conditions are actually much worse than described. In an article in the *New York Times* columnist Bob Herbert wrote "If you want to see hell on Earth, go to Zimbabwe where the madman Robert Mugabe has brought the country to such a state of ruin that medical care for most of the inhabitants has all but ceased to exist."

inviting me to teach at UZ for the upcoming *winter* quarter—once again I had forgotten my geography lesson and that Zimbabwe is situated in the Southern Hemisphere.

The proposed terms came as no surprise: teach one class, give public lectures, and meet with faculty and students. In exchange I would receive a single air ticket to Harare, a government work permit, on-campus housing, and a small living allowance. After accepting the offer and receiving authorization to purchase my tickets I booked a flight on TAP, Air Portugal, because I could later rebook and convert our ticket not just to a "twofer," as I had done on our trip to Istanbul, but this time a "threefer" with a three-day layover in Lisbon followed by a six-day layover in Cape Town, South Africa. Since this was before the days of fuel surcharges, baggage taxes, even excess pretzel charges, these two layovers added only a modest amount to the cost of the ticket. Today there would certainly be significant surcharges for adding two stops to an itinerary, but these costs would still be far less than the price of a round-trip air ticket from the United States to southern Africa.

We arrived in Cape Town in the late morning after an exhausting eleven-hour flight from Lisbon. Forcing ourselves to stay awake and adjust to local time, we took a leisurely walk around the city ending up at the classic Greek-columned South African Parliament building in Company's Garden Park, totally unaware we were about to witness a momentous historical event.

The information booth informed us that Parliament would be called into session in just a few minutes. Thinking this an interesting way to pass some time and stay awake we secured our entry passes and went upstairs to the visitor's gallery unexpectedly packed with reporters, photographers, and observers. Every seat was taken and there were numerous standees, ourselves included. Was something special happening or do South Africans have a greater interest than Americans in the proceedings of their legislature? My wife and I once visited the U.S. House of Representatives in Washington DC when it was in session. There were maybe two dozen visitors and even fewer legislators seated on the floor. The gallery hushed as President F. W. de Klerk entered the assembly, stepped to the lectern, and began addressing Members of Parliament (MPs) but, unfortunately, in Afrikaans. I thought to myself how sad I would not be able to understand a word he said, but after five minutes he smoothly, and without warning, switched to impeccable Oxfordian English. To our utter amazement, now that we could understand, he announced to everyone seated on the floor and in the visitor's gallery that his government would, effective immediately, rescind all remaining racial segregation laws still in force. At that point, the conservative Afrikaner MPs stood up, turned their backs to him, and stormed from the hall as the gallery erupted in cheers and photographers sprang to their feet to snap photos. What had begun as simply an afternoon stroll to stay awake had ended with our witnessing one of the most significant moments in African history—the official end of apartheid in the Republic of South Africa. Eighteen months after that speech, F. W. de Klerk and Nelson Mandela shared the Nobel Peace Prize at a ceremony in Oslo, Norway.

Two days later Ruth and I joined tens of thousands of South Africans, white and black, for a rousing concert organized to celebrate this joyous event. The headliner was the well-known South African musician Hugh Masekela who had left his native land to protest the Sharpeville massacre of 1960 in which sixty-nine peaceful protesters against apartheid were killed by police. This was the first time he had returned to his homeland in over thirty years.

After these historic events, our remaining time in South Africa, while full of enjoyment, felt like a bit of an anticlimax.

We flew from Cape Town to Harare and were met at the airport by Dr. Rob Borland, the head of Computer Science at the university, who took us to our accommodations, an on-campus building called the UZ Visitor's Lodge. The lodge had once been home to the president of the university, but after violent student protests in the late 1980s he felt it more prudent to be housed a bit farther from campus and a bit more removed from the reach of angry students. His large seven-bedroom home was converted into a boarding house for visiting faculty and scholars. Each visitor and spouse had a private bedroom while everyone shared the communal living room, music room, outdoor patio, and swimming pool.

Meals were provided by the lodge staff, and we ate as a group in the large, elegant dining room. Interestingly, early morning breakfast passed in virtual silence as everyone sat drinking coffee or tea, noses buried in the pages of the Zimbabwe *Herald*, a scene not unlike most breakfast tables in the United States. Lunch was a little more animated, but dinner was the highlight of the day. Cocktail hour, by the pool, began at 6 p.m., when people returned to the lodge from their day's teaching and research activities, with everyone contributing to a shared community liquor stash. Dinner followed at 7 p.m., by which time everyone's lips were well oiled and conversation and opinions flowed freely. In an ironic twist, I contributed a bottle of Chivas Regal scotch to the cache—my drink of choice—while a Scottish visitor at the lodge offered his bottle of Jack Daniel's Tennessee Whiskey!

It was a beautiful home, and we loved staying there as we were able to interact with professionals from around the world. That summer we met university scholars, government officials, and medical researchers from Denmark, Holland, England, Bulgaria, Israel, and Japan. The shared housing and lively mealtimes gave us a chance to share our latest discoveries of good places to eat, the best and cheapest shopping, and interesting destinations for weekend getaways.

Most guests at the Visitor's Lodge were there for short-term stays, usually seven to ten days. Since we were bedded down for three months, we gradually evolved into "old-timers" dispensing advice to recent arrivals on things to do and places to see. Of course, we would include ourselves in their travel plans, so we often made trips around the country with our fellow boarders. While perhaps not as luxurious as that Georgian colonial in Istanbul, the UZ Visitor's Lodge was a superb place to spend a few months, and it generated deep and lasting friendships with professionals from virtually every continent.

One topic I have studiously avoided in these pages is my experience inside the classroom with students, lectures, and labs. This was a conscious decision, as nothing would more quickly dampen interest in this narrative than a few indecipherable pages of computer science minutia such as network protocols, Matlab primitives, or Java objects. Even my wife starts to snooze if I begin waxing rhapsodic about a new exercise for my Data Structures course.

However, there is one educational concern I need to raise and immediately put to rest—the quality of students you will most likely encounter when working in either a developing economy such as Zimbabwe, at least when we were there, or a poorer third-world nation like Kenya. Of course no one would expect anything but outstanding students at a top-tier university in a country like England or Israel. Turkey, a NATO ally, could also rightfully be assumed to have good quality university programs filled with excellent students. Unfortunately, some professionals might shy away from working in countries like Kenya or Zimbabwe assuming, incorrectly, that students and colleagues will be unprepared, facilities prehistoric, and the level of instruction barely higher than that of grade school. Wrong! While some of the more costly resources—computers, research equipment, library collections—are often not at the level of a similar facility in Europe or the United States, the students were uniformly excellent, not just smart but some of the most enthusiastic and hardest working I have had in thirty-four years of teaching. There is a simple explanation.

Kenya, for example, has a population of forty million, with a larger percentage of citizens of college age (18–25) than the United States. However, the country has only nineteen public colleges and universities, amounting to one university for each 2 million residents. This makes admission extremely competitive. Top schools, like the University of Nairobi, attract the best and brightest students in the country, or at least the best and brightest who do not attend college overseas. The great majority of my students at both the University of Nairobi and UZ would succeed and, in many cases, flourish, at any good U.S. school. Furthermore, because they know they are among the lucky few to be granted admission, they are eager to make the most of their good fortune by "pumping" teachers for any and all knowledge they can. This was a pleasant change from some of the jaded and often bored students back home who treat classes as hurdles to get over on the way to a high paying job on Wall Street or Silicon Valley. Some of my most enjoyable times were the hours spent in the school cafeteria or coffee house chatting with students who wanted to continue the discussions even though class had long since ended.

This working vacation in Zimbabwe was an ideal "proof of correctness" for our commitment to the *not again* school of travel. The country has many superb game parks that provide close-up views of all the big mammals from the luxury and safety of a jeep, not unlike the many safaris made seven years earlier. However, Zimbabwe also offered experiences totally distinct from those in Kenya and Tanzania only a few hundred miles to the north.

For example, midway through our stay we drove to Great Zimbabwe National Monument, a two hundred-square-mile area of massive stone ruins constructed between the eleventh and fifteenth century, most likely by members of the Shona tribe. During the rule of apartheid, Rhodesian schools were not allowed to teach students that these magnificent buildings were designed and built by African tribesmen five hundred years before the onset of European colonial domination. That knowledge would have contradicted their racist teachings about the cultural and intellectual inferiority of blacks. Paul Sinclair, a senior archeologist at Great Zimbabwe during the time of apartheid, stated:

> Censorship of guidebooks, museum displays, school textbooks, radio programs, newspapers and films was a daily occurrence. Once a member of the Museum Board of Trustees threatened me with losing my job if I said publicly that blacks had built Zimbabwe. . . . It was the first time since Germany in the thirties that archaeology has been so directly censored.[5]

Today, the park and its structures, the largest stone buildings in Africa after the Great Pyramids of Giza, are a source of great pride to Zimbabweans and upon independence in 1980 the country, originally named after Cecil Rhodes, an English businessman who founded the De Beers Diamond Company, was renamed in honor of this historical site. The national flag contains an image of the bird carvings found on the walls and towers of Great Zimbabwe. It is an archeological treasure and one of the few extant examples of ancient African tribal culture on the continent.

We traveled to the Eastern Highlands on the border with Mozambique to hike in its high mountains and enjoy its copious displays of wildflowers and birdlife. Of course we made it to the biggest and most famous tourist attraction in all of Zimbabwe and, indeed, in all of Africa—Victoria Falls, called by locals *Mosi-oa-tonya,* the Smoke that Thunders. At 360 feet in height and more

---

5. Julie Frederikse, "Before the war," in *None But Ourselves,* Biddy Partridge, photographer (Harare: Oral Traditions Association of Zimbabwe with Anvil Press: 1990) [1982], 10–11.

than a mile in width, it is one of the largest waterfalls on the planet and one of the Seven Natural Wonders of the World. In addition to spectacular views from the unfenced rim of the chasm—if you wish, feel free to sit and dangle your feet over the edge—there are also heart stopping, Class 5 (expert level, extremely dangerous) whitewater rapids on the Zambezi River to keep you fully entertained and sopping wet.

The highlight of our time in Zimbabwe was a trip to a game park called Mana Pools, about two hundred miles north of Harare. Unknown to us prior to arrival, we heard stories from guests at the Visitor's Lodge who could not stop talking about a wildlife experience totally unlike that of more well-known places like the Serengeti and Masai Mara. Mana Pools is the only game park in Zimbabwe offering walking safaris that recreate the classic big-game experiences of the nineteenth and early twentieth centuries— before the advent of satellite phones, Land Rovers, and trucks laden with luxury provisions. Back then the only game you saw was what your guides could locate and the only provisions available were those carried on the backs of porters.

We were met at the park's front gate by our guide, Willie DeBeers, a grizzled sixty-something Afrikaner toting a massive elephant gun and missing three fingers on his right hand, courtesy of a close encounter with a spotted hyena. Each day our group of a dozen would walk for six to eight hours searching for game as Willie kept a watchful eye for unfriendly beasts to the front; the porters had our backs. Since we were on foot and without access to a locked vehicle for safety, we would stop when passing a tall stand of elephant grass to let Willie make sure nothing unfriendly was lurking in the shadows. Our daily route was not preplanned but dictated by any signs of animal life spotted by the guide— footprints, spoor, recent kills—as well as the presence of irritable beasts that require a large cushion of space between themselves and human intruders.

Observing a bull elephant while walking in the wild. A few seconds later he charged our group.

One morning we happened across a massive bull elephant not more than a few hundred feet ahead, bellowing and scraping the ground with his right front leg. Willie informed us this behavior meant he was about to charge.

Right on cue he did, all four tons of him, heading straight for the group at full gallop. I froze in utter terror until he came to a dead stop not fifty feet away. Willie laughed and informed us he could tell from the animal's demeanor this would be a "false charge," and that the elephant would stop before reaching us. We were told to move slowly backward from the angry beast—still standing in front of us—and everything would be just fine. He had let the elephant charge to give us some excitement and provide a great story for friends and family back home.

Three weeks later a story appeared on the front page of the

Zimbabwe *Herald* about a UZ geography professor trampled to death by a rogue elephant at Mana Pools. I can only assume this animal was uninformed about Willie's rule requiring all elephants to clearly indicate a false charge. This was a little too much for me in the way of recreating nineteenth-century realism, but Willie was right about one thing. I did end up telling this story to family and friends as soon as I got back home.

When we returned from Zimbabwe the following September I shared stories of our adventures with Prof. Paul Tymann, a close friend and co-author of a computer science text. Paul is a professor at the Rochester Institute of Technology in Rochester, New York, and, like Ruthie and me, had long dreamed of going on an African safari. He had never considered, in fact was not even aware of, the concept of a working vacation until I related my experiences in both Kenya and Zimbabwe and described how I was able to plan and finance these trips. After listening to my stories and determining this was something he truly wanted to do, he contacted Dr. Rob Borland at UZ and carefully followed the steps I laid out for him during our talks. He was soon rewarded with a teaching offer, and the following summer Paul was comfortably ensconced at the UZ Visitor's Lodge reliving many of the African adventures Ruth and I had experienced only twelve months earlier, including that walking safari at Mana Pools. Yet more proof there really isn't anything unique about me when it comes to living and working overseas.

This last story highlights an excellent way to locate a working vacation and a strategy that often works far better than a random cold call to an unfamiliar place. If you know any colleagues who have recently returned from an overseas stay, talk with them about their experiences, accommodations, and the school, agency, or institute where they worked. If they speak positively about their time overseas then ask for the name and address of a contact person and send that individual e-mail inquiring about the possibility of your own working vacation, being sure to include your friend's name.

It would also be a good idea for your colleague to send an enthusiastic letter of recommendation directly to the location or give you a copy to attach to your e-mail. If the people at this site were pleased and satisfied with your friend's work, they should be amenable to a visit from someone recommended by that individual, just as I had personally recommended Paul. This approach does not qualify as a "cold call," like those described in earlier chapters, since this institution has already demonstrated an interest in hosting overseas visitors, resulting in greater likelihood of success. In essence you are no longer scattering seeds randomly but planting them in ground already well watered and nurtured by the work of others.

One person that summer was to play a very prominent role in my future travels and to change my entire approach to planning and financing overseas adventures. Jon Pearce is a professor of computer science at San Jose State University in California and was working at UZ while I was there, but he was visiting under the auspices of a U.S. State Department Fulbright Scholar Grant. I had heard about the Fulbright program and had even received mass mailings from their Washington DC office. Unfortunately, I treated these flyers like all other spam and junk mail—I deposited them in the recycle bin or trash folder. I was to learn from Jon that this was a big mistake as the Fulbright Program is a mecca for overseas travel and the single largest source of working vacations in the world. Over the next fifteen years I would more than make up for that oversight, and the Fulbright office and I were to become the very best of friends.

A few years later I had a chance to repay Jon for the favor he did in opening my eyes to the multitude of opportunities available from Fulbright. He and his wife wanted to live and work in Turkey, and he remembered that I had worked there the year before we met in Zimbabwe. I happily shared my experiences at Bogazici University, provided contact information for the chair, Prof. Kuru, and e-mailed the school a supportive letter of recommendation on Jon's behalf. Three months later I received a letter from Jon and his wife Ronna informing me they were comfortably settled in Istanbul, living in a lovely Georgian colonial home overlooking the Bosporus.

CHAPTER 7

Ask, but Ye Shall Not Always Receive

Reality check: The last three chapters described my resoundingly successful cold-calling exploits—all sevens, blackjacks, and cherries across the bar. This unfailing good fortune might lead you to believe that traveling the world on the other guy's dime requires nothing more than a contact name, cleverly worded e-mail, and a positive outlook, with a few academic letters after your name thrown in for good measure.

Yes, I had good luck in response to my blind calls, but I would be remiss if I did not share some of my more abject failures if only to convince you not to lose hope when the inevitable disappointment strikes. I learned this important lesson from a writing instructor who walked into class the first day, introduced himself, and proceeded to boast he had published forty articles in magazines, guidebooks, and Sunday travel sections of major metropolitan dailies.

Since my own total of published travel articles was zero, I was duly impressed. But then this successful writer opened his briefcase, removed a stack of papers three inches high, held them up for all to see, and announced he was also the proud recipient of more than three hundred rejection letters. His moral was clear—if you plan on becoming a professional writer you need a thick skin and a short memory. We can adapt his advice to our situation. If you plan on applying for a working vacation you will need those same two attributes as well as patience, perseverance, and a Gandhian willingness to accept rejection without losing hope. Let me provide some examples.

Almost every traveler fantasizes about life on a remote South Pacific island—a thatched-roof cottage ringed by date palms, white sand beaches, and turquoise colored surf. Depending on how erotic you like your dreams, it may include gorgeous Polynesian women in multicolored sarongs or hulking, bare-chested young men paddling outrigger canoes. You laze in a hammock sipping a piña colada from a hollowed out coconut shell while. . . . OK, you get the idea.

I wanted to live this idyllic lifestyle, not just dream it. I had already fulfilled wishes to go on an African safari, swim in the Dead Sea, and roam the ancient bazaars of Istanbul, so why not a tropical isle? The beauty of the working-vacation concept is that you are free to choose your own fantasy, and this was mine. So, on a particularly cold and snowy Minnesota winter day, I drove to our local bookstore and purchased the Lonely Planet's *Guide to the South Pacific*. Each night before bed I would read about the island nations that dot the Pacific waters until I could discourse intelligently about the cultures of Fiji, the handicrafts of New Caledonia, the birdlife of Samoa, and the beaches of Tonga.

Eventually I found that one perfect Eden, the place visited so often in my dreams—the tiny island nation of Palau, about five hundred miles due east of the Philippines. To say that Palau is beautiful is to damn it with exceedingly faint praise. It is a tropical wonderland both above and below the water, with pristine ivory beaches and some of the finest snorkeling and diving to be found anywhere in the world. The Lonely Planet's photographs were a globe-trekker's dream, and it did not take much on that cold January night to convince Ruth and me that this pearl of the Pacific should be our next working vacation destination. We were ready to buy snorkels, swim fins, and lay in a stash of SPF 50.

The only institution of higher education in the Republic of Palau is Palau Community College (PCC), a two-year vocational school. This type of career-oriented junior college is completely different in curriculum and philosophy from my school in St. Paul, a highly selective four-year liberal arts college. However, when it comes to locating a desirable working vacation such differences are immaterial. I was not going there to carry out high-level research or puff up my academic résumé. I was not searching for a new career or a position to keep me occupied until retirement. I simply wanted a place where I could work, learn, grow, and spend a few glorious months. If PCC offers courses that I am qualified to teach, then I can offer to teach them. Don't be overly picky when it comes to evaluating working vacation opportunities—focus on the location and the cultural experience, not the institution.

I revised my standard cover letter to make it more applicable to a junior college—for example, offering to present workshops on new developments in the first two years of the computer science curriculum. I e-mailed my new letter, along with course syllabi and workshop abstracts, to the head of the IT department and sat back and waited. Like clockwork, a "You have mail" icon appeared in my inbox within the week with a response from PCC. However, this time its contents were not at all what I had hoped for or wanted to see:

Dear Dr. Schneider

Thank you for your inquiry but we have no need for a visiting teacher at PCC at this time. Best of luck.

Terse, direct, right to the point. It certainly exuded a tone of "don't bother following this up with another request. We don't have anything."

This type of response is, unfortunately, all too familiar to any struggling artist, dancer, or writer who has submitted an unsolicited manuscript, answered a cattle call audition, or pitched a movie script. It is also a response that will become quite familiar to anyone who uses cold calls to locate a working vacation. The majority of time you will get either a polite rejection or no response at all.

The trick now is not to give up hope. There is a plan B, but before starting down that path send a polite thank-you saying you are sorry it did not work out and if anything comes up in the future to please keep you in mind. The great majority of time this courtesy is a waste of time and the likelihood is that nothing will come of it. However, like those throwaway words to my lunch mate Morris from Imperial College, you never know when, against all odds, someone will dig out your letter from the detritus of their inbox archives and give you a call. E-mail is free and composing a polite "boilerplate" response takes only a few seconds, so it is worth your time and effort to send off a quick thank-you to keep the lines of communication open.

OK, what next? What *is* plan B? Simple—when searching the Web to locate schools or institutions where you might apply, don't limit yourself to a single site. Instead, locate the name of *every* place in the country or region that might use your skills because they 1) use English as the medium of communication, 2) have a department or division in your field of specialization, and 3) are located in a place where you would consider living for an extended period of time. Then prioritize this list and contact the schools or institutions in priority order.

In my case I used the Web to identify three possibilities in the South Pacific that met all my criteria:

1. Palau Community College
2. College of Micronesia
3. University of the South Pacific

All three institutions had IT programs and offered courses I would enjoy teaching, all three used English for classroom instruction, and all were in luscious tropical locations with fascinating cultures that would certainly satisfy my idyllic fantasies. Although I really wanted to live and work in Palau, upon receiving the rejection letter from PCC I tried again, first sending e-mail to the College of Micronesia in the Federated States of Micronesia, and then to the University of the South Pacific on the island nation of Fiji. No dice at either, and I was now zero for three. In fact, the latter two schools never even sent a rejection letter—not a rare occurrence. If you haven't received a response in two or three weeks double check that the names and e-mail addresses are correct and resend your inquiry letter along with all attachments. If you don't hear a second time, give up. They are not interested.

OK, plan B was a failure, but it is still not time to throw in the towel as there is also a plan C. It is now time to broaden your horizons and locate schools in other countries or other parts of the world that might provide you and your family with a similar, although not identical, social and cultural experience. All too often we focus so intently on obtaining that perfect position at one particular school in one city or country, we overlook other regions of the world that could offer an equally enjoyable, not to mention rewarding, adventure.

For example, if your dream is to work in Singapore, but that carefully crafted e-mail to the National University of Singapore is a bust, consider schools in Malaysia, its next-door neighbor with a closely related culture and history. If you are dying to live and work in France but that did not work out, what about nearby Francophone Belgium as an interesting alternative? Are those letters to schools in Mainland China going nowhere? Consider applying to colleges and universities in Taiwan. What about a working vacation in Iceland when Denmark, Sweden, and Norway all say no? When considering sites for a working vacation it is important to be creative, inclusive, and flexible. The smaller the candidate pool the less likely your chance of success.

In my case, I decided to consider not just locations in the South Pacific but the Indian Ocean as well. We don't usually think of the Indian Ocean in terms of glorious getaways, but island nations such as the Seychelles and the Maldives could easily hold their own in any tropical beauty contest with their better-known Pacific cousins such as Tahiti, Fiji, and Hawaii. A few years later, after much time, effort, and rejection, success finally arrived as Ruth and I spent six glorious months on the island of Mauritius, a coral-rimmed Indian Ocean paradise just off the coast of Madagascar, an idyllic tropical adventure I describe in detail in Chapter 9.

The moral here is to expect rejection, not let it get you down, and have a follow-up response at the ready. First, consider other institutions in the same country or region that meet your language, program, and location requirements. If that does not work consider alternate countries or regions that might offer a similar cultural experience. The cost of these inquiries is insignificant— perhaps a few hours of research and a few minutes of typing. In the "olden days" (pre-Internet) each attempt at contacting an overseas school involved days or weeks of waiting for a snail mail inquiry to arrive on the other side of the globe and a snail mail response to slowly trickle back. In that environment contacting a large number of institutions was an agonizing and completely unrealistic process. E-mail and the Web have changed that, and it is now quick and easy, not to mention free, to contact a large number of schools, agencies, or research centers trying to achieve one positive response, with the ultimate payoff for that single success being a glorious overseas work experience on someone else's dime.

My second example is quite different although the result, utter failure, is the same. A few years back I read an article in the local newspaper about the establishment of the Royal University of Bhutan (RUB), the first university in this tiny, isolated Himalayan kingdom that, until recently, had been closed to Western visitors. Some people claim Bhutan was the inspiration for the fictional valley *Shangri-La* described in the 1933 novel *Lost Horizon,* by the British author James Hilton. It is a magical, mysterious country of Buddhism and alpine beauty. Now that it is open to Western travelers and had just established its first institution of higher learning, it sounded like an ideal candidate for a cold call as well as a unique and exciting place for a working vacation.

I sent e-mail to the head of computer science at RUB and in just a week received an enthusiastic response. The school had recently created an IT program and would love to have me come for one semester, teach two or three computer science courses, and consult on future directions for this infant program. I checked with my school administration and learned that if I submitted a formal request I would be granted a one-semester unpaid leave of absence.[6] I then responded to RUB that their proposal sounded fine. The chair wrote back he would take this idea to the Dean for a final decision, and not one week later I received a lovely letter from the Dean containing a formal invitation to join the faculty of RUB for the following fall semester. E-mails flew back and forth as we agreed on plans for the classes I would teach, public lectures I would give, and consultations I would have with the Minister

---

6. Getting an unpaid (or reduced pay) leave of absence is often easier than you might imagine. In my case the school could save the cost of my salary and either choose not to replace me or hire a temporary and far less expensive adjunct professor. Many institutions find that granting short-term unpaid leaves to their professional staff is a wonderful way to help balance the personnel budget.

of Education on K-12 technical education. Everything was moving smoothly, with the only issue not yet discussed and approved being the financial details of the visit.

After a month or so dancing around the topic, I wrote the Dean a demure letter saying I did not want to seem overly materialistic but I would like to know how they planned to compensate me for the work I would be doing. Their response, coming almost instantaneously, was devastating:

Dear Dr. Schneider

I am so sorry for what appears to be a serious misunderstanding. We do not have any funds available and were under the impression that you were coming to the Royal University of Bhutan as an unpaid volunteer, donating your services to the school. I sincerely apologize for this unfortunate misunderstanding.

That was it. No air ticket, no housing, no food allowance, not even a complimentary taxi ride from the airport. Nothing. Four or five months of full-time work without any remuneration, either from my home school or the overseas host institution, was not remotely possible. No matter how much I might scrimp and no matter how much I might receive for renting our house, foregoing all salary from Macalester while receiving no compensation from RUB would leave me almost destitute. In one brief instant my Himalayan travel balloon had deflated and crashed in flames.

The moral of this example is don't start shopping for that new travel bag, fancy 10X binoculars, or cool hiking boots until everything is agreed upon and the teaching contract is signed, sealed, and safely ensconced in your inbox. Sometimes the final hiring decision is the responsibility of a single person who can agree to all contractual and financial terms on the spot. (That had been my previous experience.) In other countries a number of approvals, sometimes from different groups, need to be discussed and nailed down before the deal is set—gaining approval of the administration and department, obtaining a government work permit, agreeing on an appropriate workload, and negotiating a mutually acceptable financial offer. Any one of these steps can become a speed bump that sends you flying off the road.

If that fatal bump does happen, then your exit strategy is to move to plans B and C described earlier. When bad things happen don't fold the tent and slip quietly into the night but, instead, try some of those other places that may be similar in history, geography, and culture. For example, just a few years after that Bhutan fiasco, I was able to obtain a grant to teach for two months at the University of Kathmandu in Nepal, Bhutan's Himalayan neighbor to the west and itself a breathtakingly beautiful mountain nation. And, in fall 2009 I finally received that long dreamt of invitation to live and work in Bhutan, an adventure described in detail in Chapter 13.

Just remember that if you keep trying, and sometimes trying and trying and trying, good things can happen. Failure is simply one step in the overall process, not the final outcome.

CHAPTER 8

The Man from Arkansas

J. William Fulbright was a United States Senator from Arkansas for thirty years, from 1945 to 1975, not exactly someone you would expect to impact the traveling life of an educator at a small Minnesota college. But he did, quite profoundly in fact.

During his long and distinguished career, Fulbright was deeply committed to the principles of world peace, global understanding, and the supremacy of international law, nurtured in part by his years at Oxford University under the auspices of a Rhodes scholarship. While serving in the Senate he fought to uphold these principles, supporting creation of the United Nations; opposing the Vietnam War, described in his 1966 book, *The Arrogance of Power*; and serving fifteen years as Chair of the Senate Foreign Relations Committee.

However, Fulbright's historical legacy was not established by any of these noteworthy achievements but by a single bill he co-authored in 1946 creating an international exchange program that would ultimately bear his name—the Fulbright Scholarships. The program's goal is to foster global understanding through the international exchange of students, faculty, and skilled professionals. The list of distinguished Fulbright alumni includes prime ministers, cabinet officials, diplomats, scientists, physicians, and business leaders as well as representatives of the arts, such as *Catch-22* author Joseph Heller, poet Sylvia Plath, and the Emmy and Tony Award winning actor John Lithgow.

The Fulbright Program, housed within the U.S. State Department but administered by the Council for the International Exchange of Scholars (CIES), has grown rapidly since its inception and now operates in 150 countries. In its sixty-plus years the number of people impacted by the program is staggering—about 105,000 U.S. citizens have received grants for overseas travel, while 175,000 international students and scholars have been awarded funds to come to the United States, and these totals are growing by 5,000 to 6,000 annually. This is certainly not a program whose mailings should be discarded, unopened and unread, as I had so casually done.

Since 1980 and my initial working vacation in London, I had assumed full responsibility for finding and funding our family's overseas adventures. I scoured the Web as well as magazines, newspapers, and journals for host institutions; I made the cold calls; I negotiated terms of the visit; when necessary I located housing in the host country; and I made all necessary educational arrangements for our children. It never occurred to me to let someone else, let alone a U.S. government agency, do much of that work for me. That is, until I met Prof. Jon Pearce who sat me down and set me straight.

Although Jon and I were both visiting faculty at the University of Zimbabwe, I was there by dint of my own cold-calling efforts while he was there on a Fulbright. What possible difference did that make? Well, for starters, Ruth and I were living at the UZ Visitor's Lodge while Jon and his family resided in a lovely three-bedroom home paid for by his grant. I was getting a nominal living allowance, while he was receiving a generous salary. I had to cover the cost of my wife's airline ticket to Zimbabwe, while air tickets for Jon's wife and children, as well as the cost of shipping his books and research materials, were paid for compliments of the U.S. government. Private school tuition for his two young children, which, if you remember from Chapter 3, can be quite steep, was also fully subsidized by his grant.[7] His family was even invited to the July 4th gala at the U.S. Embassy in Harare hosted by the Ambassador, while Ruth and I sat home explaining the significance of our national holiday to lodge residents and staff. As you can see, there was a huge difference between our two visits.

When we returned from Harare in fall 1992, following some informative and eye-opening discussions, Ruth and I had come to understand and appreciate that the Fulbright Program offers numerous opportunities for intellectually and culturally rewarding travel within a safe, comfortable, and pleasant working environment. I knew it was a program I needed to investigate much more closely.

What my investigations revealed was that the traditional Fulbright Scholar grant, the oldest and most well-known of its many programs, provides a large number of attractive and well-funded working vacation possibilities, but for two reasons it may not be a perfect fit for everyone. First, the great majority of grants last either one semester (four to six months) or one academic year (eight to ten months), more than the three-month leaves I had been taking, and for some, too long a time to be away from home because of work or family circumstances. Second, the time lag between initial application and the start of the overseas visit can be as much as twelve to eighteen months, necessitating both long-term planning and an understanding employer with an expansive time horizon. This is quite different from the one-week to one-month acceptance/

---

7. As one example of the educational costs a Fulbright grant will cover, the Harare International School in Mt. Pleasant, the suburb where the UZ is located, charges $8,800/year for students in grades K-5 rising to $12,500/year for students in high school.

rejection period for a typical cold call, and it is a delay that often cannot be accommodated by one's employment schedule.

If either of these issues constitutes an insurmountable problem then you might consider the two- to six-week Senior Specialist Award. This is a new class of grant (described in detail in Chapter 11) created for the express purpose of providing shorter overseas visits for those who cannot get away for four to ten months at a time. Alternatively, you could continue the cold-call strategy of the previous three chapters or opt for one of the alternate approaches discussed in Chapter 14, "It's Your Turn Now." However, if these two issues are not a cause for concern (for Ruth and me the possibility of a longer visit was a highly desirable feature), then a Fulbright Scholar Grant could be the perfect match for you and your travel fantasies.

The process of applying for a Fulbright Scholar grant, covered fully at www.cies.org/us_scholars/us_awards/, can be rather daunting. This chapter will focus on the nuts and bolts of the process in order to give your application the greatest chance of success, a success I happily achieved four times; those adventures form the story line of upcoming chapters.

The Fulbright Scholar Program is open to any U.S. citizen. Academics should hold a Ph.D. or equivalent terminal degree such as an M.D., J.D., Ed. D., or M.F.A. Professionals not affiliated with a college or university, such as engineers, artists, K-12 teachers, physicians, architects, business leaders, lawyers, or clergy, are not required to hold a terminal degree but must be able to demonstrate, in the words of the grant guidelines, "significant public accomplishments and recognized professional experience." Grants are awarded for teaching only, research only, and joint teaching/research, where "teaching" implies anything from large lectures to one-on-one tutoring or clinical sessions, and "research" can range from highly theoretical laboratory research to applied work such as advising schools and government agencies on policy and planning. The great majority of Fulbright grants do not require foreign language proficiency as all work is in English. A few countries, mainly in South America or Francophone Africa, require fluency in a second language, and the applicant must demonstrate competency via examination or certification from a native speaker.

The "holy book" of the Fulbright Scholar Program is the *Catalog of Awards*, published online at www.cies.org/us_scholars/us_awards/AwardsCatalog.htm every March 1, and listing all awards for the coming year by discipline and country. There are usually about 800 grants in 140 countries, although these numbers fluctuate due to civil unrest or health concerns that would disqualify a country from participation in a given year.

I would await the March 1 publication date with the same anticipation as birthdays or Chanukah, and when it appeared I would pour through it as carefully and lovingly as if it were the Neiman Marcus holiday catalog. It is a book of fantasies and dreams, describing teaching jobs in New Guinea, Sri Lanka, and Portugal; research positions in India, Morocco, and China; and far-flung scholarly postings to Namibia, Malta, and New Zealand, all provided by our government in total comfort and safety.

Obviously not all 800 positions will be a match for your skill set, so the initial step is to determine which of the many possibilities is the best fit. The awards catalog includes forty-five disciplines ranging from agriculture to zoology, with all the usual suspects—medicine, computer science, biology, engineering, and business. However, the breadth of interests in the catalog is impressive and includes grants in archaeology, dance, film studies, library science, linguistics, religion, and dozens of other subjects, both popular and little known. Start by generating a list of all awards in your discipline and, if applicable, any closely related discipline in which you are fully qualified to work.

If you are a non-teaching professional there is a separate category entitled "Awards Open to Non-Academic Professionals." There are about fifteen to twenty entries per specialization, although that number varies greatly by field. For example, the first catalog that I ever looked at had sixteen entries in computer science, forty-four in American History, but only five in Dance. However, even that number can be misleading as a single catalog entry may include multiple identical awards.

The following paragraphs show two typical Fulbright Scholar grant entries, one describing three identical computer engineering lecturing awards in India, the other a single lecturing award in Macedonia, in either Business or Computer Science:

▶ **South and Central Asia|India**

Communication and Computer Engineering
Award #9467

Category: Lecturing

Number of Awards: 3

Deadline: August 1, 2008

Grant Activity: Teach graduate and undergraduate students, participate in curriculum and faculty development.

Specialization(s): Mobile communication, RF antenna design, satellite, optical communication, Internet security, microelectronics, digital signal processing, offshore structures, information security or compiler design, depending on host institution

Additional Qualifications: Ph.D. and at least 2 years experience. Professionals with research publications will be considered for one affiliation.

Location: Birla Institute of Technology and Science; Punjabi University or National Institute of Technology

Length of Grant: 4 months to 6 months

Starting Date: July or August 2009

Comments: Obtain additional information on awards from CIES. Prior to submission of an application, scholars should contact host institution representatives for details of departments and universities. In the order of listed institutions, contact: (1) Prof. R.N. Saha, dean, at edd@bits-pilani.ac.in, or visit www.bits-pilani.ac.in; (2) Dr. Manjeet Singh Pattern at pattarms@ieee.org or mspattar@gmail.com, or visit www.punjabiuniversity.ac.in; or (3) Dr. G.R.C. Reddy, director, at director@nitc.ac.in; or visit www.nitc.ac.in. Furnished guest housing will be provided at some locations.

Grant for Three Awards in Computer Engineering in India

<u>Europe|Macedonia</u>

For supplemental information on this country please click <u>here</u>

Business Administration or Computer Science
Award #9310

Category: Lecturing

Deadline: August 1, 2008

Grant Activity: Teach approximately two undergraduate and/or graduate courses per semester. Assist with curriculum and junior faculty development.

Specialization(s): For specialists in business administration, developing entrepreneurship or any area of business administration. For specialists in computer science, any area of computer science or information technology.

Language: English should be sufficient for lecturing; however, interpreters will be provided for classes if needed.

Additional Qualifications: Ph.D. strongly preferred; however, non-academic professionals with teaching experience will be seriously considered.

Location: Ss. Cyril and Methodius University or South East European University

Length of Grant: 4 months to 9 months

Starting Date: October 2009 or February 2010 for one-semester grants; October 2009 for academic-year grants

Comments: Contact persons for this award are: Xhevair Memedi, Secretary General at South East European University (SEEU): x.memedi@seeu.edu.mk, university Web site: www.see-university.edu.mk; Ms. Marija Cenevska, University of Ss. Cyril and Methodius: mcenevska@ukim.edu.mk, www.ukim.edu.mk; Blake Childs, project development officer, State University of Tetovo: Blake.Childs@yahoo.com, www.unite.edu.mk.

Grant for a Single Award in Either Business or Computer Science in Macedonia

Next, for each entry determine whether or not this award is a viable choice by asking yourself if this is a destination where you and your family would enjoy living and working for anywhere from a semester to an academic year. Some people might consider nine months in Macedonia to be the dream trip of a lifetime; others may view it as punishment for some unknown transgression. If the grant passes this first hurdle, take a look at the area(s) of specialization to see how well your skills match the request. For example, the India grant is quite specific, asking for technical specialists in a narrow set of fields—mobile communications, RF (radio-frequency) antenna design, Internet security, etc.—while the Macedonia grant specifies nothing more than "any area of computer science or information technology." If you are unsure whether you possess the necessary skills, each listing includes a contact name and address where you can write or e-mail for additional information, specifically information about the nature of the work a successful applicant will be expected to perform.

If your background and abilities are a good match then look next at Qualifications. Sometimes a Ph.D. is required, other times only "preferred." Sometimes the grant is limited to experienced academics, other times non-academic professionals with appropriate experience will be seriously considered. See if there is a language requirement other than English. In both of the above examples, there isn't. Finally, check the grant's starting date and duration to determine if they mesh well with your schedule. It does no good to have a spring sabbatical if the grant insists you start work in the fall.

When you have finished your analysis place this award into one of two groups—inappropriate or a potential choice—and repeat for all the entries in your field and any related fields. At the end you will have produced a short list of possible awards. Because of the hurdles each entry must clear—country, specialization, qualifications, language, duration, starting date—this may be a very short list with only one or two entries. It may be even shorter, namely zero, if not a single award passed all the required tests. If that happens don't despair quite yet as there is one more possibility.

In addition to the forty-five disciplines explicitly included in the award's catalog, there is a catchall forty-sixth, entitled "All

Disciplines." Football enthusiasts are familiar with the NFL coach who, when deciding which college player to draft, announces he is going to select the best athlete available, regardless of position. Schools do the same thing. Rather than informing the Fulbright Commission that they would prefer an ecologist, violinist, or civil engineer, they declare they will be happy to accept the best U.S. scholar available, as in the following award entry from Italy:

> ▸ **Europe|Italy**

All Disciplines (Lecturing)
Award #9283

Category: Lecturing

Deadline: August 1, 2008

Grant Activity: Lecture at graduate level in the scholar's area of expertise and participate in ongoing activites of the host department, i.e. curriculum development, graduate student advising, etc.

Language: Lecturing is in English. Conversational Italian is helpful.

Location: Applicants must arrange affiliation and include letter of invitation.

Length of Grant: 4 months

Starting Date: To be arranged with host institution; between October 2009 and January 2010

Comments: Information about Italian universities can be found at www3.unibo.it/infostud-altreuni/eurouni/itauni/italia.htm. For infromation about grant details, please contact Barbara Pizzella, program officer, U.S.-Italy Fulbright Commission, bpizzella@fulbright.it.

All Disciplines Award from Italy

This entry asks the successful applicant to lecture at the graduate level in "the scholar's area of expertise" without any restrictions on what that area of expertise should be. In cases like this your evaluation of the award is no longer based on whether you are a good match for their needs, as none are listed, but simply whether this is a destination of interest to you and your family and whether all other criteria are a good match as well. With a little luck, when you finish dissecting the "All Disciplines" group your list will no longer be empty. If it is, then it is time to cry *No mas,* chill out until the following March 1, and start again with the new catalog.

Now you face the single most difficult step in the application process—narrowing your list of choices to exactly one. The Fulbright Scholar Program is somewhat unusual in that you must apply for a single award—no back-ups, no second chances, no plan B. There is no way to tell the review board that if your first choice is unavailable you would be more than happy to accept the second-place finisher. All travel eggs must be dropped into a single award basket so you must select this basket carefully.

Your choice will be based on three factors: 1) whether it is a discipline-specific or all-disciplines grant, 2) how well your skills match the award specifications, and, finally, 3) how attractive this destination will be to other applicants.

Given a choice, all other things being equal, opt for a discipline-based award over one from the "All Disciplines" category. With the latter you run the risk of being blindsided by a world-class specialist from a totally unrelated discipline. You might be the best RF antenna professional in the applicant pool and, if the competition were limited to that one area, you would be boarding the plane as we speak. However, with an "All Disciplines" selection you could lose out to a virtuoso ballet dancer, a world-class expert on Afghan literature, or a specialist in sustainable agriculture, since you are theoretically competing against them all. If an "All Disciplines" grant is the only possibility on your list, then go for it, but if there is an option available in your specific field of expertise, it would be preferred.

Of course, the single most important contributor to success is your ability to convince the host school that you have all the necessary skills to handle the job. Therefore, select the award that allows you to make the strongest evidentiary case for your professional abilities. Even though you may truly want to apply to country X, don't be tempted if your experience and background in the skills requested by country X are a recent development, casual hobby, or a secondary area of interest. You will be competing against professionals from around the country so your application has to clearly convince the host institution you are without question the best person to fill that position.

Telling you to select a discipline-specific grant in which you are eminently qualified is not exactly earth-shaking advice. However, there is a third factor influencing your final choice, a factor that has nothing to do with you or the heft of your résumé; instead it has everything to do with *where*. The number of people applying for each of the 800 grants listed in the catalog fluctuates wildly. In plain English, everyone wants to go to France and Italy; far fewer want to end up in Azerbaijan or the Republic of Sudan.

The Fulbright Scholar Program does not publish statistics about the number of academics and professionals applying to each country, although they do for student awards—statistics for the number of student applicants for each country in the last award cycle are available at us.fulbrightonline.org/thinking_competition.html. These numbers are quite revealing. For example, in one year in the European region 341 students applied for postings to Germany, 190 for awards in France, 9 for Bulgaria, and a single, lone individual sent an application to Albania. Anecdotal evidence indicates that Fulbright Scholar grant applications for academics and professionals would follow a similarly skewed distribution.

The identity of the most popular destinations comes as no surprise, but the scale of those differences—factors of 30, 60, 100, even 300—indicates how carefully you must select your award destination. European countries such as England, France, Italy,

Spain, Germany, and Switzerland are enormously popular; Asian/Pacific destinations such as China, Japan, India, and Australia are fiercely competitive; popular South American destinations like Chile, Brazil, and Argentina also have large numbers of applicants, perhaps twenty or more for each opening. There are approximately 140 countries in the awards catalog, and I have just named a dozen or so of the most competitive, with another twenty or thirty that could easily be added to that roster. But that still leaves more than a hundred potential destinations, many of which can offer the successful applicant a fascinating, once-in-a-lifetime professional and cultural experience in complete safety and comfort. For example, my Fulbright awards have been to Mauritius, Malaysia, Nepal, and Mongolia, while friends and colleagues have received grants to live and work in Iceland, Sri Lanka, Malta, Ukraine, and Zimbabwe. Not one of these was a destination that anyone ever regretted having chosen. Best of all, these are all destinations that can be significantly less competitive and give applicants a realistic, rather than remote, chance for success.

The lesson of these numbers is that when making that critical decision about your destination, temper those passions for the south of France, the Amalfi coast of Italy, or the beaches of Rio with the sober realization of how difficult it can be to receive a Fulbright to these immensely popular areas. Remember the "feast or famine" structure of the application process—if you don't get your first choice you get nothing at all. So, open your mind, and the awards catalog, to the possibility of a somewhat lesser-known, but still safe and inviting country. Give serious thought to destinations a little further off the main road that you may not have considered, or even heard of, at the start of the application process but that, with a little reading and study, could become more and more attractive.

You've thought long and hard and have made that crucial decision. You have selected a single country and a single award and are ready to start preparing your application. Each award has a deadline date that is "drop dead" fixed—ten minutes late and you might as well fold your tent and go home. Make sure to have everything completed and sent to Washington DC well in advance of the deadline—usually August 1, but double-check the award for which you are applying—included in the catalog listing.

When preparing the proposal you won't be flying blind as there is a wealth of information at www.cies.org/us_scholars/us_awards/ApplicationInstructions.htm, and I won't bother duplicating that excellent advice here. There are also many helpful hints and suggestions at www.cies.org/us_scholars/us_awards/Tips.htm. These two Web sites contain information about steps in the application process not discussed here, such as selecting professional references and, if necessary, obtaining a letter of invitation from the host institution. Read and digest these instructions fully before putting fingers to keyboard.

One of the most common errors in the application process can seriously dampen your chances for success. When describing their skills and experiences applicants often downplay or even omit achievements some high-level professionals consider "trivial pursuits" that take time away from the "real" work of scholars and university professors—grants, patents, solo performances, research papers, and Ph.D. students. In reality these grade-A achievements, while certainly impressive, can sometimes be among the least important items included on a Fulbright application form, especially in developing nations whose educational and consulting needs are much more prosaic.

During one Fulbright visit I discovered that what had tipped the scales in my favor during final review was a line on my application stating that I had worked closely with high school teachers helping to design age-appropriate computer science courses for grades 9–12. This turned out to be of great importance to my host school as they were in the process of developing pedagogical materials for high school technology courses. I did not mention that some of my colleagues had berated me for wasting time on this "silly high school stuff."

Another Fulbright came my way because I had authored an introductory text. My host institution did not care about the content of the book or even want to use it in a course. However, in their value system publishing a university-level textbook is a great honor and considered an achievement of great intellectual prowess. I presented a well-attended faculty workshop on textbook writing and publishing, even though, according to the tenure code of my previous school, the time I spent on undergraduate textbook writing was more indicative of a misplaced set of academic priorities.

When preparing the application, don't limit yourself to the usual litany of major accomplishments—papers published, invited talks given, grants received. Of course you will include these on your application, but be creative and remind yourself of the many other contributions to the discipline that, although they may carry little or no weight with regard to tenure, promotion, or salary, could be of seminal importance to a Fulbright review committee. These accomplishments could include professional offices held; local honors and awards; consulting with governments, primary/secondary schools, or businesses; books, software, and pedagogical materials authored; new courses developed; and faculty workshops presented. Any of these seemingly minor contributions could become your ace in the hole. To paraphrase, but invert, an old saying, "*Do* sweat the small stuff."

Non-academics should heed the same advice—don't limit your résumé to only major achievements such as inventions, patents, promotions, awards, or concert performances. In addition to such "big successes" be sure to include "smaller triumphs" such as designing a popular Web site, working with underrepresented groups, organizing and running professional meetings, or creating and implementing a new management structure. Any one of these achievements could be of interest to a potential host country and tip the scales in your favor.

When you have completed and mailed the forms, or, more correctly, e-mailed them as the application process is handled online, there is nothing to do but sit back and wait, and you may end up waiting quite a while. Fulbright reviews are a two-step operation. In the first step, a review committee from CIES winnows the number of applicants to produce a short list, perhaps two or three candidates for each award. If you make this list you will be informed sometime between October and January for grants with August 1 deadlines.

It can be disheartening to receive an official letter from Washington that starts out "We are pleased to inform you . . ." but then realize it is not an award announcement but simply a notice that you have qualified for step two. In the second step the short list of candidates for each award is sent to the host country, which makes the final selection and informs Washington of its choice. You will receive a second letter sometime between February and June, as much as ten months after submitting your application, and this will be the official notice informing you whether or not you have been awarded a Fulbright Scholar grant for the upcoming academic year.

If the answer is positive, let the celebrating and planning begin. The Fulbright Scholar grant benefits vary based on the transportation and living costs in the host country and whether or not you are traveling with dependents. The schedule of benefits for each grant is included in the awards catalog. The following is an example of the Benefits entry for a Fulbright Scholar grant to Zimbabwe:

Benefits

Stipend: $2,640–$2,860 monthly base stipend, according to the <u>standard base stipend</u> formula.

Maintenance: <u>Standard maintenance</u>. For 2007–2008 the following was provided: $900–$1,200 per month, based on the number of dependents, plus a housing allowance or a one-time allowance of $1,000 for refurbishing and repair of university provided housing.

Travel/Relocation: <u>Standard travel/relocation</u>. For 2007–2008 the following was provided: $6,400 for the grantee; additional dependent travel allowance of $3,600 for one accompanying dependent, $7,200 for two or more dependents.

Tuition assistance: Up to $25,000 per family for grades K-12 is reimbursed for two or more accompanying dependent children for full adcademic year, with maximum benefit of $12,500 per child. Amount adjusted for shorter grant periods. Reimbursement based on actual cost of tuition and fees only or home schooling materials. Requests to cover higher actual amounts for tuition and fees only will be considered but cannot be guaranteed.

Benefits Package for a Fulbright Scholar Grant to Zimbabwe

Grant benefits fall into five categories. *Stipend* is your monthly base salary and varies according to academic rank and grant type but is usually about $2,800 per month. (These numbers will certainly grow in the coming years. Check the latest Fulbright catalog for the current dollar amounts.) *Maintenance* is a monthly allowance to cover living expenses—such as housing, food, and laundry—in the host country. This varies according to local costs and the number of dependents. The Zimbabwe grant, above, provides a maintenance allowance of $900–1,200 per month, as Zimbabwe has a low cost of living. Other examples of maintenance are $1,400 for Brazil, $2,400 for China, and $2,700 for Germany. Taken together, the monthly stipend and maintenance allowance provide an income of about $3,500 to $5,500 per month.

When these funds are added to any monies received from the rental of your U.S. home, they should provide an adequate and comfortable income stream. *Travel/Relocation* expenses cover transportation costs to and from the host country, and they are typically quite generous. For example, the Zimbabwe grant includes $6,400 if traveling alone, $10,000 if traveling with a single dependent, and $13,600 if you are going with spouse and one or more children. As a second example, the travel budget for China ranges from $3,550 to $8,150 depending on family size. This should be more than adequate to cover round-trip airfare from your home to the host country, and any remaining funds can be used for travel throughout the region during the period of your Fulbright. Most grants provide *Tuition Assistance* to cover the costs of private schooling. For example, the Zimbabwe grant provides up to $25,000 annually per family for K-12 education, which was enough to fully cover the private school costs for Jon's two young children. Finally there are miscellaneous *Other Benefits,* which could include such things as funding for teaching and research activities, or overweight shipping costs for books and educational materials. In the case of Zimbabwe, the grant includes a one-time housing allowance of $1,000 for home repair and refurbishment of university-provided housing.

After carefully following the guidelines just laid out and waiting nervously for almost nine months, on April 16, 1995, I received a letter from the U.S. State Department that began "We are pleased to inform you . . ." and ended with ". . . the recipient of a six-month Fulbright Scholar grant to the Republic of Mauritius for the period July 1 to December 31, 1995." I had done it! No more cold calling. I had graduated from the ranks of working-vacation telemarketer to someone officially anointed and supported in my overseas travel by the U.S. government. Ruth and I were heading to the tropical island paradise of Mauritius, located six hundred miles due east of Madagascar, in the Indian Ocean.

Now it's time to move beyond this administrative litany of catalogs, benefits, specializations, and qualifications. You just heard you have received that long-awaited grant—let the Fulbright adventures begin!

CHAPTER 9

Fantasy Island

Mark Twain, the noted American author and humorist, wrote in his 1897 travelogue *Following the Equator: A Journey Around the World,* "You gather the idea that Mauritius was made first and then heaven, and that heaven was copied after Mauritius." I could only agree as I gazed out at lush tropical vegetation, turquoise-colored water, and wispy casuarina trees lining miles of white sand beaches. Could Palau have been any more beautiful?

The fleeting two-and-a-half month interlude between that April award notification and our July 1st arrival was filled with pre-departure hubbub. I hired replacement faculty to teach my courses and signed up renters to live in and care for our house. This latter task was more of a struggle than usual since, for the first time, tenants would arrive in the warmth and sunshine of July but remain until after New Year's Day. Paying December and January Minnesota heating bills can be a painful experience not to mention a hard sell.

Another pre-departure activity was our required attendance at a two-day orientation conference in Washington DC for all

Fulbright recipients traveling to Africa which, by accident of geography rather than history, culture, or economics, includes Mauritius. There were presentations on AIDS, sanitation and health care, tropical maladies, political instability, and tribal conflicts. My wife and I faithfully attended every session, listening ever so politely, even though the biggest concerns facing Fulbrighters in Mauritius, a safe, stable, and relatively wealthy island nation, were of a quite different ilk—sunburn, traffic jams, and tracking beach sand into the house.

Finally, with our required tasks all duly completed, we departed Minneapolis on June 29 for a destination that could not have been more distant. When using the globe in our den to show friends where we were headed—they would confuse Mauritius with Mauritania—I noticed an interesting geographic phenomenon. If you were to stick a pin from Minneapolis through the center of the planet and out the other side, the country nearest that exit point would be Mauritius, isolated and remote in the far reaches of the Indian Ocean. We were, quite literally, traveling to the other end of the Earth. It would be a journey of almost 11,000 miles, not a pleasant prospect for those who detest long flights; this is when you start gulping down sleep-aids and muscle relaxants to make the long trip bearable. Our legal drug of choice was Halcion, a powerful prescription medicine that knocked us out in Amsterdam and left us semi-comatose until we awoke for landing in Nairobi. It worked perfectly and made this ever-so-long expedition seem almost pleasant. (In 1992, President George H. W. Bush gave the drug a bad reputation when he used it on an overnight flight to Tokyo, and the next day proceeded to "upchuck" in the lap of Japanese Prime Minister Miyazawa.)

Despite our exceedingly generous travel budget, we decided to fly coach. On a trip of this length it is tempting to opt for the far greater luxury and comfort of first class, even though the cost is significantly higher. If you can tolerate it, I urge you to choose coach and move to the rear of the aircraft. A Fulbright travel allotment is not lost if you don't spend it on your original flight to and from the host country. On the contrary, any remaining funds are available for the remainder of the grant period. In our case the $3,000 saved by flying coach paid for sightseeing excursions to Madagascar and Reunion Island, trips that would not have been financially possible if we had originally traveled first class.

Finally, on the morning of July 1, two days after departing the heartland of the United States, Ruth and I looked down on our new home, a place that only eleven months earlier I could not have located, pronounced, or even spelled. Just prior to landing, an announcement came over the speakers saying, "Would passenger Schneider please identify himself." Fearful that my papers were not in order or that I had already made some huge diplomatic *faux pas*, I pushed the call button and was told that my wife and I would depart first while the other passengers were held in their seats, probably wondering why this sloppily dressed couple back in coach were being given the royal treatment.

As we walked down the ramp I understood our being singled out, for there on the tarmac, parked next to the aircraft, was a U.S. Embassy car, with two staffers waiting to pick us up, retrieve our baggage, and whisk us through customs without our suffering such "indignities" as overloaded baggage carts, long waiting lines, or groping body searches by overzealous immigration agents. It was then I came to realize that this visit would be quite different from our earlier trips. We weren't in Kansas anymore.

Even though we were exhausted from this two-day travel ordeal and only wanted to see a shower and a soft bed, our gracious hosts insisted upon showing us a few of the island's most popular sights. We stopped to view multicolored coral reefs, an extinct volcanic crater, and a hilltop vista encompassing virtually the entire country—really not that impressive when you consider Mauritius is twenty-five miles long by thirty miles wide, making it only slightly larger than Hennepin County, my home county in Minnesota. Finally, after the fourth or fifth "... and there on your left ..." (I'm not exactly sure as I fell asleep somewhere along the line) our hosts relented and took us to the hotel that would be our temporary home until we located a permanent residence.

This was our second "Fulbright moment," after that red carpet airplane exit, as the car pulled into a five-star beachfront resort complete with waterfront bungalows, cabanas, pool, and an outdoor terrace encircled by palms for *alfresco* dining. The Embassy had prepaid six nights, meals included, to give us time to recover from jet lag and find appropriate accommodations. They had even made arrangements for a realtor to pick us up and show us around but, in a most thoughtful gesture, not until two days later while we lazed on the beach and reset our internal clocks. It took only a single day to find a lovely two-bedroom apartment, near the university, with a patio overlooking both mountains and ocean. Although it was available immediately we chose to delay the move for three days to savor every last minute of our luxurious, not to mention complimentary, oceanfront quarters.

After settling into our new home I proceeded to move into my office at the University of Mauritius. The university, founded in 1965 and home to 8,000 students from undergraduate to doctoral, is a top-notch institution of higher education, one of the finest on the African continent. Although virtually unknown to Americans, and Europeans for that matter, it attracts young men and women from countries throughout eastern and southern Africa. Like those earlier experiences in Turkey, Kenya, and Zimbabwe, over the next six months I was to become thoroughly impressed with the academic skills of the students, almost all of whom would do very well at my own institution in St. Paul.

I was also to learn that the well-worn phrase "island pace of life" is not some stereotype created by Hollywood scriptwriters to caricature languid tropical cultures. At about 3:45 p.m. on that first day at work, everyone around me began closing books, packing up belongings, and heading for the exits as security guards roamed the hallways turning out lights and locking doors. I discovered that university buses depart promptly at 4:00 p.m. for all corners of the island—with no later options—and since most students, staff, and faculty do not drive, everything pretty much shuts down. By 4:05, what was once a campus building bustling with intellectual life had become as quiet as a funeral hall. This was so different from my own campus, and probably most others in the United States, where faculty members agonize over grading, lecture notes, and research articles until well into the late afternoon and evening. As I walked to my car toting a briefcase filled with work I planned to finish that evening, I was humorously chastised by colleagues who asked, "Why do you bring work home? That is what tomorrow is for." There was a good deal of logic in that telling comment, and my briefcase did not come out again for the duration of the stay.

So, what to do with those leisurely late afternoon hours after school lets out but before dinner is served? One possibility was to sit on our patio with friends and neighbors, sip a cool drink, and watch the sun slip into the ocean—rather easy as our terrace faced due west. Many quiet evenings were spent in just that fashion, but an even more attractive alternative was something called Flic en Flac, quite possibly, with apologies to Hawaii, Tahiti and other glamorous island getaways, the most beautiful place in the world. Flic en Flac, derived from the Dutch phrase *Fried Landt Flaak* meaning "free and flat land," is a pristine, palm-strewn beach on the western coast only a few short miles from our apartment. The site sits about 800 feet below our hillside home in Quatres Borne, so the drive there is downhill into the setting sun, with a broad expanse of palms, sand, and ocean in full view for the entire trip. We were definitely not in Kansas anymore.

The reason behind the popularity of sunset watching and beach excursions, not to mention drinking, is that in Mauritius there is simply not much else to do. The slow pace of island life applies not only to work but one's social life as well. This is a quiet, laid-back, early-to-bed country that does not go in for live concerts, bars, raucous music, or late night clubbing. The home is the center of virtually all social activity, and the primary form of entertainment is having friends and family over for libations, a meal, and pleasant conversation. In the entire country—note the word *country*, not city—there was not a single movie theater, not a single orchestra or concert venue, and no live theater.

A few years after we left, a shopping mall was built in Port Louis, the capital city, which included a movie theater and bowling alley. How I would have killed for that in 1995. The upshot of this mellow lifestyle is that, unless you want to go to bed every night soon after the sun goes down, you had better make good friends who include you in their evening's drinking and dining activities.

Fortunately, this was not a problem. We became best friends with Vimala Appayya, a young faculty member in my department. She lived only one mile away and, as she did not own a car, I drove her to school each morning and back home again in the afternoon. I helped her with English speaking skills that, although grammatically perfect and fine for teaching, came across in everyday conversation as a bit stilted and formal since the language spoken at home was not English but Creole, a French dialect common throughout Mauritius. To learn colloquial American English she had checked out some old mystery novels from the local library (think Nero Wolf) and was reading them to gain what she considered a more "current" vernacular. However, after hearing her refer to a female friend with loose morals as a "brazen hussy" I convinced her she sounded more like a 1930s *noir* Hollywood movie than a street-savvy American. From that point on our commuting trips turned into slang study sessions, including words not always appropriate for mixed company.

In exchange for carpooling and "ESL" (English Slang Lessons), Vimala and her family took Ruth and me in like adopted children and had us to their house for meals, games, and conversation. During these visits we learned about Mauritian history, culture, and traditions, while they listened intently to our stories about life in America. We exchanged fish curry and chocolate chip cookie recipes; we explained Judaism and the Torah while joining them in Hindu celebrations such as *Diwali,* a joyous festival where neighbors bake sweets and give them to friends and neighbors. We also benefited from this friendship in an unexpected way. Soon after our arrival, Vimala's cousin was arrested for DWI, lost his driving privileges, and became our source for a reasonably priced six-month car rental.

One of the biggest differences between Mauritius and our previous working vacations, especially England, was the number of friends and family who came to visit or, more accurately, did not come. During our three-month sojourn in London we were overwhelmed with drop-ins, and our guest room was in constant use. However, when you are on the other side of the world separated by a two-day journey not to mention a $2,500 airline ticket, the number of visitors willing to make this trek is far, far less. Therefore, making friends with locals was crucial, especially as we were going to be there six months.

In addition to neighbors and colleagues, a great way to meet locals, if you are an academic, is through your college's Alumni Office. Before we left Minneapolis I stopped at the Macalester Alumni Center for the names and addresses of any alums, regardless of major or year of graduation, currently residing in Mauritius. Surprisingly, there were three—a classical Indian dancer who performs for tourists at five-star hotels, a member of the Mauritian Parliament, and a Hindu *pandit,* a scholar learned in Sanskrit and Hindu philosophy and religion. We became good friends with all three, as they were eager to reconnect with their *alma mater* and hear stories about what was happening on campus and in the Twin Cities. They were also excited to introduce us to aspects of Mauritian culture and politics that would otherwise have remained utterly unknown.

For example, the Hindu *pandit* invited us to join him at a *Haldi* where he was officiating. The *Haldi* is a Hindu cleansing and purification ceremony held the night before a wedding where guests dine on vegetarian fare served on banana leaves and eaten with your fingers. Then, in a spirit of celebration and gaiety, smear the future bride and groom with a bright yellow paste made of turmeric, rosewater, and sandalwood.

After a lengthy and frank discussion on race relations in Mauritius and the United States, the parliamentarian described the unique Mauritian voting system called the "best-loser representation" about which Ruth and I were totally ignorant. Mauritius is a parliamentary democracy with seventy members, but only sixty-two of these seventy seats are allocated to winners of the popular vote. The remaining eight seats go to the *losing* candidates who received the most votes and who are members of one of the

Traditional Mauritian food served on banana leaves at a Hindu Haldi ceremony. Our daughter, Rebecca, is sitting between us. Vimala is on the far right.

island's three minority groups—Muslim, Chinese, and African. These best-loser seats ensure that every ethnic community has representation in the federal legislature and cannot be shut out of the political process.

On a continent where tribalism is rampant and honest elections are a rarity, this tiny island nation has, for over fifty years, used an electoral system that formally guarantees legislative representation to all ethnic groups. I can only imagine the furor that would ensue if the U.S. Congress set aside a few seats in our House of Representatives to ensure that African-Americans, Latinos, and Asian-Americans were minimally represented.

When living and working in a remote destination where few friends or family will make the long journey, remember that alums or previous employees are a wonderful source of local contacts. Before leaving home find out if your school or company has any graduates, past workers, or previous visitors living in the host country. If so, look them up. They will most likely be happy to see you, eager to welcome you, and excited to share experiences that you would not have on our own.

Finally, if you are in the country on a Fulbright grant, another source of contacts is either the U.S. Embassy or the local Fulbright Commission Office. Every nation that accepts Fulbrighters is required to have a grantee support system in place. In the fifty or so largest countries this support is provided by the Fulbright Commission, a local office that offers information for students and scholars applying for grants to the United States as well as support and assistance for U.S. grant recipients working in the country. Smaller destinations, such as Mauritius, that do not have a separate Fulbright Commission, provide this support through the Public Affairs Office of the U.S. Embassy.

In countries such as England, France, or China where, at any instant of time, there will be thousands of Americans on holiday, study away, or business, the U.S. Embassy is often too busy to spend time with a single visiting professor. Due to tightened security you may not even be allowed inside the embassy building. However, in smaller countries the arrival of a Fulbrighter can be a significant event, and the staff is usually happy to include you and your family in many of their social and cultural activities.

That was the case in Mauritius where we became good friends with a number of embassy employees and were invited to numerous events. For example, the husband of the Deputy Chief of Mission was a South African Jew, and they celebrated *Rosh Hashanah,* Jewish New Year, by hosting a dinner for every Jew in the country, all twenty-two of us.[8] Most of the guests were non-Mauritians who had come to the island on holiday, fallen in love with a local, married, and settled down. Owen Griffiths, for example, is an Australian Jew who married a Mauritian woman, moved to the island, and opened La Vanille Crocodile Park, where he farmed Nile crocs for viewing, eating, and turning into shoes and handbags—not an occupation I run into very often in either New York or Minneapolis. The following month we celebrated Thanksgiving with embassy staff and other visiting Americans by dining on turkey, cranberries, chestnut stuffing, and pumpkin pie flown in from the United States in the diplomatic pouch—and you foolishly thought it was used only for "Top Secret" documents!

The most memorable embassy event occurred near the end of our six-month stay. As mentioned earlier, there were no cultural venues on the island other than tourist shows at the big hotels—no orchestra, no live theater, no concert halls. My wife and I enjoy theater and classical music and frequently attend concerts in

---

8. The first synagogue in Mauritius, *Amicale Maurice Israel,* was dedicated on May 23, 2005, ten years after our visit. The building includes a small chapel, office, kitchen, and communal hall seating about 200. Religious services are held once a month, usually led by a visiting rabbi from South Africa or the French island of Reunion. The fascinating history of this tiny but active Jewish community is described at www.africanjewishcongress.com/MAURITIUSCONG.htm.

Minneapolis. However, for five and a half months our Mauritian social lives had consisted of dinner parties, conversation, reading, and watching the sun set over Flic en Flac—extremely relaxing and totally stress-free activities, but lacking in the aesthetic and intellectual stimulation we appreciated at home and on previous overseas trips.

Then we received a call inviting us to a concert sponsored by the U.S. Embassy for guests and officials of the host country as a gesture of good will and a demonstration of American musical talent. The soloist that night was a classical guitarist, and the sonorous music of Bach, Mozart, and Albeñiz was like cool water to parched throats. After such a long period of cultural deprivation, the opportunity to hear a skilled virtuoso literally brought tears to our eyes. Four years later when Vimala was in the United States on her own Fulbright, we attended a concert by the Philadelphia Symphony Orchestra. Even though she was twenty-nine years old it was her first classical concert, and she also cried upon hearing those melodious sounds.

I've given you a number of helpful hints for meeting locals and making friends in a land where you don't know anyone and will have few, if any, visitors; let me now caution you about one local group that you might wish to avoid even though they will almost certainly welcome you with smiles and open arms—the expatriate community, usually just called expats. The dictionary defines an expatriate as someone who has withdrawn from residence in or allegiance to his or her own native country. Expats can come from anywhere and be there for any reason. Many of us know stories of black musicians and artists who left America in the 1920s and 30s because of discrimination, moved to Paris, and became American expatriates. Many Southeast Asians moved to America after the Vietnam War and became expatriates to avoid political reprisals for their assistance in the American war effort.

Here, however, I am not referring to just any expats, but one group in particular—the Brits and other past and present members of the "Empire," especially Aussies, Kiwis, South Africans, Scots, and the Irish. Ruth and I have lived in a number of countries that were once British possessions and are now part of the Commonwealth—Kenya, Mauritius, India, and Malaysia, among others. In every one there is a large, active British expat community that welcomes new English-speaking members from the "colonies" which, of course, we were until 1776.

Although there are many warm, friendly, and interesting expats living all over the world, wherever we have traveled it seemed that the two primary activities of this British diaspora are to recreate small pieces of their homeland and bemoan their wretched existence in this remote backwater of the globe. These expats love to sit in mock English pubs with names like The Moldy Frog or The Goat and Whistle; throw back pints of Guinness, Fosters, or Bass Ale; and complain about the heat, food, bugs, traffic, local soccer team, or anything else that does not compare with what they left behind in Auckland, Adelaide, or Aberdeen. They talk endlessly about the "good old days" while doing their best to avoid learning the local language and integrating into the local community. They often form private expat organizations where reminiscences can be shared on a regular basis with like-minded individuals.

Unaware of exactly what we were getting into, Ruth and I attended one of these events, the monthly meeting of a popular running and drinking club called the Hash House Harriers. The group was founded by British officers and expats in Malaysia in 1938 and has expanded to 1,700 chapters on seven continents. Of the sixty attendees at this meeting, fifty-nine were Americans or Commonwealth citizens, while the lone Mauritian was an expat spouse who did not appear too happy to be there. The day's activity involved jogging through the woods following a series of clues nailed to trees, sort of a cross between orienteering and a scavenger hunt, ending at a picnic site where we ate a lunch of hamburgers, chips, and cold beer while singing English drinking songs. It felt more like a fox hunt in Worcestershire or a pub in Cornwall than a social gathering in the middle of the Indian Ocean. It seemed that the goal of this club was not cultural immersion but cultural isolation. Needless to say we never went again.

Our experiences at this expat get-together were so different from those evenings with the Appayya family during which a couple of Midwestern American Jews and some Mauritians of Hindu and Tamil extraction shared their traditions, learned about each other's religion, and cooked and ate each other's food. We much prefer the latter. You don't travel to a country with a strange, new culture only to hang out with people who look like you, eat like you, and behave like you. That defeats the purpose of these working vacations, which is to grow intellectually and culturally and become a more informed global citizen. Beware of falling into an "expat trap" in which you surround yourself exclusively with friends from home and isolate yourself from the community in which you are living. Ruth and I decided that if we want to drink Guinness and sing English pub drinking songs we would simply return to London.

Our six-month stay in Mauritius was twice as long as any prior working vacation, and that added length led to an unexpected problem—a bored spouse. When you spend two or three months in London, Jerusalem, or Istanbul, the city's many sights will keep you fully occupied, and boredom should not be a problem. However, six months in a small country with one spouse working five days a week can leave the other spouse itching for something more to do, and this usually means trying to find a job. In almost all cases, though, you are going to bump into legal restrictions that prevent you from doing just that. For example, in many countries entering on a tourist visa prevents you from accepting paid employment.

In the case of a Fulbright grant, the spouse with the award receives a visa that allows the grantee to work and receive a salary.

The other spouse gets a tourist visa that does not permit any form of paid employment. This is true for most other grant types as well. In many countries working without the appropriate papers or permits is a serious crime that can land you in jail or, at a minimum, have you deported. So, what to do?

The answer is simple—you may not be able to work for a salary, but you are certainly allowed to volunteer your time and your services. In 1995 Ruth was a certified preschool teacher. Although she was not permitted to take a regular classroom position, she volunteered two days a week at a Mauritian preschool and became best friends with the school principal, Ms. Rada Valaydin and her husband Sumu. Ruth helped out at the school and traveled with Rada to preschools around the country evaluating their programs and making suggestions. Not only did Rada and Sumu become our dear friends, but Ruth remained active and intellectually involved in the educational life of the country. She met the First Lady of Mauritius, a teacher before becoming a political celebrity and very interested in early childhood education. She invited Ruth to write a report on her experiences entitled "My Views on the State of Preschool Education in Mauritius" and submit it for review and consideration, which she did.

No matter what your area of specialization there will always be a volunteer opportunity that can take advantage of your skills. If you are a health professional you can volunteer at a local hospital or clinic; if you are a psychologist or counselor, offer your services to an orphanage, group home, or prison; musicians and artists could provide free music lessons or art enrichment classes for children in the neighborhood. If none of these apply, then offer to help students at a local public school with English language reading and speaking skills. Just remember, no matter where you are located there is never a shortage of good work that needs to be done.

Even though this working vacation was twice as long as the others, our late December departure date seemed to arrive just as quickly. The number of close friends we had made in the last six months rivaled those of any prior trip, and the round of going-away parties was endless—computer science colleagues, the Appayya family, the Valaydins, embassy employees, even the crocodiles. Even though our apartment building did not have a thatched roof—a bit impractical since it was eight stories high—and it was not right on the ocean, although, to borrow the infamous words of the former governor of Alaska and onetime vice presidential candidate Sarah Palin, we could see it from our house, my fantasy to live on a tropical island paradise had been fully and completely realized. I would not have changed a single thing except, perhaps, to have the island's first movie theater, bowling alley, and shopping mall completed a few years earlier.

We departed Mauritius on December 29, but this time not through Nairobi and Amsterdam, as was the case with our arrival, but via Mumbai. Even though we had already made recreational side trips to Madagascar and Reunion Island, there was still enough money left in our travel budget to cover the cost of adding a two-week layover in India to the return itinerary. (Are you beginning to appreciate the advantages of flying coach instead of first-class?) We spent two weeks exploring the western coast of the country—Goa, Bangalore, Mysore, and Cochin—before returning to Mumbai and making the long *schlep* home, arriving exhausted and jet-lagged but with film cartons and memory banks overflowing with pictures and stories.

Just as there were innumerable going-away parties there were equally as many welcome-home ones. Many of our friends and family had been to England, Israel, even Turkey, so on our return from those trips they were not all that eager or excited to hear stories or see pictures, which I could understand. (I never impose wedding, travel, or grandchildren photos on anyone without permission given willingly and without duress.) However, six months on a remote tropical island in the Indian Ocean is a bit more out of the ordinary, not to mention a couple of weeks in India, and it piqued their curiosity. We were swamped with requests to exchange dinner and drinks for a slide show and story hour, and were more than happy to oblige.

One of my professional colleagues, Prof. Joel Adams of Calvin College, was on the receiving end of these shared stories. Two years later he, his wife, and two small children were comfortably settled into their beachfront home in Mauritius–additional proof that the adventures described in these pages are not unique to me, and the ideas and advice contained in this book along with some simple, direct action can lead to a truly transformative travel experience.

When the hoopla finally settled down and a somewhat regular routine settled into our lives—a routine that sadly did not include either Flic en Flac or a 4:00 p.m. quitting time—Ruth and I ruminated about this longer overseas experience. We both agreed that spending six months, rather than two or three, gave us more time to settle in, make good friends, and become an integral part of the local community. We did not feel as rushed as we had on earlier trips. We also agreed that we would not want to spend any additional time away as after six months we were beginning to miss our home, family, and friends in Minneapolis. For us, a working vacation of a four- to six-month duration, approximately one academic semester, seemed to be the ideal length of time, and we were determined to try and repeat this half-year-long overseas work experience again as soon as possible.

I dug out the Fulbright Scholar grant rulebook and studied the guidelines listed under the heading "Required Interval of Time Between Grants." We were ready; the question was when would Fulbright be ready for us.

CHAPTER 10

A Most Discriminating Culture

Rule 624.2; paragraph one, of the official Fulbright rulebook states:

> . . . recipients of a basic Fulbright grant are eligible to receive a second Fulbright grant five years from the date of completion of their previous grant.

Ruth and I were adhering to the letter of the law as we stepped off the plane at Kuala Lumpur International Airport to begin our second Fulbright adventure, this time in Malaysia. It was 12:01 on the morning of January 1, 2001, exactly five years *and one minute* after the official December 31, 1995, completion date of that first grant in Mauritius and at the very moment ushering in the new millennium—let's not rehash that tired old argument about whether the new millennium occurred on Jan 1, 2000, or Jan 1, 2001. It was obvious what was happening as fireworks exploded overhead, cell phones jangled, and passengers hugged anyone standing beside them, shouting Happy New Year in Bahasa Malaysia, English,

Mandarin, Hindi, Thai, and a multitude of other languages utterly unrecognizable.

Our first Fulbright in Mauritius had been such a rewarding and pleasurable experience we were determined to apply for another as soon as it was permissible under the rules. In the interim, Ruth and I enjoyed summer holidays in Ecuador, the Galapagos, Eastern Europe, Chile, and Easter Island. However, since these trips were financed out of our own pocket, they violated the basic premise of this book and won't be discussed further except to say they were enormously informative and thoroughly enjoyable.

When the new Fulbright catalog appeared on March 1, 1999, listing grants available for the 2000–01 academic year, I carefully picked through it searching for awards beginning on or after January 1, 2001, the earliest allowable starting date. And there it was. Grant #5913: an eight-month lecturing position in Malaysia starting January 1. The award was for someone to teach undergraduate computer science classes, advise on curriculum, and help nurture the fledgling IT program at Multimedia University in the planned city of Cyberjaya, thirty miles southwest of the capital, Kuala Lumpur (KL).

To compete economically against the four "Asian Tigers"— Singapore, Hong Kong, South Korea, Taiwan—in 1997 the Malaysian government established the high technology enclave of Cyberjaya. They hoped it would attract world-class IT companies and be an incubator for entrepreneurs and developers in chip design, telecommunications, software development, and related high-technology fields. The voracious employment needs of these companies would be met by graduates of Multimedia University, or MMU as it is called, just down the road. As I was to hear many times during my visit, the plan was for MMU to be to Cyberjaya what Berkeley and Stanford are to Silicon Valley.

The position sounded ideal, met all my application criteria— discipline specific, good fit with my abilities, not an overly competitive location—so I filled out the application, waited an agonizingly long thirteen months, and eventually received that prized "Congratulations, you have been awarded . . ." letter from the Fulbright office in Washington DC. I was two for two in the game of grantsmanship and batting 1.000.

Ruth and I flew coach directly from Minneapolis to KL, as this time we decided to squirrel away the bulk of the generous travel allowance for side trips to some of the fascinating and less-often visited destinations sprinkled throughout Southeast Asia. The downside to this decision was that it required nineteen hours of flying with only a brief layover in Osaka, Japan, to break up the ordeal. One of these days I really need to consider a working vacation in Winnipeg, a short forty-five minute hop from Minneapolis.

We arrived in KL at that auspicious millennial moment and were met by staff from the U.S. Fulbright Commission, this time at the front door of the terminal rather than on the tarmac. (Too bad. I had enjoyed that red-carpet entrance.) As we exited the airport we had our "welcome to the tropics" moment as we went directly from the bone-chilling, over-air-conditioned 66-degree indoor temperature of the airport (as well as virtually every other public building, we would soon find out), to the sauna-like 100-degree heat and 95 percent humidity outside; it hit like a slap to the head, especially since we departed Minnesota with the temperature standing at a brisk and invigorating -1 degree Fahrenheit.

Since we were arriving in January, I had foolishly thought the climate might be a bit less oppressive than the steamy, strength-sapping summers for which Southeast Asia is so well known. How wrong. In Malaysia, the only way to recognize the change of seasons is to check a calendar, not a thermometer. Every day is the same—hot and humid with torrential afternoon rainstorms arriving precisely at 4:00 p.m. I would quickly learn to appreciate the pleasures of a cool afternoon gin and tonic enjoyed under a shaded umbrella, my one condescension to British colonialism.

Fortunately, our hosts drove us directly to the hotel without stopping for sights along the way, most likely because there is precious little to see in the remote exurbs of KL. Like in Mauritius, our hotel was a luxurious five-star lodging lacking only the glorious beachfront sunsets of Flic en Flac, and, as with that first grant, our hosts had graciously made arrangements for a realtor to pick us up two days later and show us rental apartments.

It was then we realized we needed to make an important decision and one that you may also face during working vacations—where to live. The schools where I had worked previously were located either in the central city or a close-in suburb so our apartment selection was based solely on choosing the nicest unit without worrying about exactly where it was located. However, new schools often cannot acquire sufficient space for a campus within the central city, so they move out to the farthest reaches of the metropolitan area where land is available and cheap. This was the case with MMU, thirty miles south of downtown, in an undeveloped area of rubber tree farms, palm oil plantations, and little else. We would face a similar decision in Nepal a few years later when teaching at Kathmandu University, located in the small village of Dhulikhel, twenty-two miles northeast of the city over a winding mountain road. In these cases it is no longer simply a case of finding nice accommodations, but also deciding where those accommodations should be.

In situations like this the operative principle has to be, *make your housing choice based on where you want to live, not on where you work*. A thirty-mile commute may not be enjoyable, but it is far preferable to returning home after work, stuck in the middle of nowhere and facing a sixty-mile round-trip, perhaps through heavy traffic or on poor roads, to enjoy any type of recreational, social, or cultural activities in the central city. Additionally, although the Fulbright spouse will have work and colleagues to occupy weekday mornings and afternoons, the other spouse will be faced with the daily prospect of long drives into the city or long hours doing nothing,

We ended up renting a beautiful two-bedroom apartment in a complex that offered a swimming pool, workout room, laundry services, and poolside bar. It was situated in the trendy and affluent urban neighborhood of Bangsar, the "SoHo" of KL, an area filled with shopping, restaurants, bars, night markets, and easy access to downtown, only two miles away.

Don't fall into the mindset of thinking that your home must be close to work. Choose a working-vacation residence the same way you select a neighborhood in the United States—in an area of a city that offers you and your family the most enjoyment, convenience, and safety for the duration of your stay. My sixty-mile round-trip commute, while unpleasant, was temporary, and the otherwise-convenient location afforded us seven months of easy access to culture, shopping, and nightlife. The close-in location

Our lovely apartment in KL. On most of our working vacations we ended up with housing of this quality.

also allowed my wife to participate fully in Malaysian society, volunteering in an ESL class at a local school and taking an Asian art course at a nearby studio.

During those first few days, Ruth and I were to discover a fascinating but disconcerting aspect of Malaysian culture that would come to dominate our morning coffee and evening dinner conversations—and become a controversy that almost caused me to be thrown out of the country. Malaysia, like Mauritius, is a multicultural society composed of 65 percent Malay, all of whom are Muslim; 26 percent Chinese; and 8 percent Indian. The official government line is that there is no discrimination among races and Malaysia is a country where all cultures live in harmony, respect religious and ethnic differences, and enjoy the diversity of food, dress, music, and holidays that each group brings to the table. Sounds great, but the reality is quite different.

As I made the long drive to work on that first day I passed an apartment under construction, at least twenty stories high, with a mammoth advertising banner draped from roof to ground announcing "Rentals Available, Call XXXX-XXXX, Malay Only." Those last two words, "Malay Only," struck me immediately as I tried to imagine a building in any U.S. city of the 21st century advertising on a twenty-story high sign for all to see, "Rentals Available, Whites Only." How could such blatant discrimination be permitted in a country where diverse cultures live in supposed equality and harmony?

When I returned home eager to share what I had seen my wife beat me to the punch, breathlessly relating what happened when ordering cable-TV for our apartment. One of the questions the salesman asked was "Are you Malay?" When she asked what possible difference ethnicity could make when purchasing cable services he told her that *Bumiputras,* the local term for ethnic Malays, receive a discount on their monthly bill, while Chinese, Indians, and others do not. Things were becoming stranger—not only did there appear to be officially sanctioned discrimination in housing but television watching as well. We were to encounter this phenomenon many more times in those early days, including a local dentist who announced that she gives Malays a discount on fillings, bridges, and crowns. What was going on?

What was happening, as we soon found out, was Article 153 of the Malaysian Constitution, drafted shortly after the country's independence in 1957. This controversial law establishes the "special position" of the Malay people and grants authority to the King for maintaining and safeguarding these privileges:

> It shall be the responsibility of the Yang di-Pertuan Agong [elected Monarch] to safeguard the special position of the Malays and natives of any of the States of Sabah and Sarawak . . . in accordance with the provisions of this Article.

Article 153 constitutionally enshrines the preeminence of Malays over citizens of other ethnic backgrounds with regard to certain governmental and business services. It also led to the passage of laws defining these privileges more precisely such as the NEP, New Economic Policy, which mandates a minimum 30 percent share of the economy be set aside for Malays, and the NDP, National Development Policy, which sets quotas for Malays with regard to civil service jobs, housing, and public education. Furthermore, the constitution makes it technically illegal for anyone to publicly question this law or discuss its repeal.

Article 153 was written into the constitution to address a real and serious problem existing at the time of independence—the wretched economic status of the Malay community. Although they were 65 percent of the population they controlled only 4 percent of the nation's wealth. While Chinese and Indian Malaysians were overwhelmingly professionals, academics, businessmen, and tradesmen, the Malay were mostly subsistence farmers and unskilled laborers. It was believed that without some protection expressly included in the new constitution this economic imbalance would continue and even worsen, eventually leading to violence and social instability. Article 153 was meant to be temporary, giving Malays time to gain equal economic footing with other groups, and the original plans called for it to be repealed fifteen years following its ratification. Instead it became an integral part of the national psyche and was still in effect when we arrived in KL, forty-four years after independence.

While paying a little more for HBO and being charged extra for teeth cleaning are not particularly burdensome problems, it was a markedly different story at school. Each of my two classes had fifty students, with an ethnic makeup close to the constitutionally mandated allocation of 55 percent *Bhumiputra* and 45 percent other, meaning Chinese and Indian. Initially I was oblivious to this ethnic mix. At Macalester I routinely have white, black, Asian, Jewish, Gentile, gay and straight students in the same class, and I consider this racial, religious, and cultural diversity to be one of the joys of teaching at a progressive liberal arts college. However, at MMU it was hard to be oblivious when, in my first class, only thirty-six students showed up for lecture—every one of the Chinese and Indian students but less than two-thirds of the Malay.

This pattern continued throughout the semester with Malay absenteeism running 30–40 percent, rising to 70–80 percent in the days immediately preceding school holidays. The Chinese and Indian students agonized over each point on an assignment and, when completed, begged for an opportunity to earn extra credit. Most *Bumiputras* chose not to do the homework or violated class rules and copied the work of others. The average Chinese/Indian score on the midterm was 84 percent; Malays averaged 45 percent, below the minimal passing grade of 50. It was like teaching two distinct classes within a single room—one to overachieving undergrads, the other to remedial high schoolers.

When I shared my experiences with colleagues they gave a world-weary "We know all about that" shrug, having faced the identical situation in their own classes for years. The higher education quota guarantees every Malay student a seat at a public four-year university regardless of high school performance, while the civil service quota ensures a secure, full-time government job upon graduation regardless of GPA or rank in class. Article 153, passed with the best of intentions and with Malay economic equality as its laudable goal had, like many other "well-meaning solutions," generated a totally different and unexpected set of problems. These set-asides had led to the end of individual initiative and the loss of any motivation to work hard and improve one's lot in life. The Malay community had become a ward of the state living almost exclusively off the singular status and special privileges written into the Constitution fifty years earlier.

My teaching colleagues wanted to speak out about conditions in the classroom but were well aware of what can happen to those who question the status quo. Tenure cannot protect you from dismissal or worse, so nothing was said, nothing was done, and academic life at MMU continued unchanged. It was at this point I asked myself the most difficult question I have faced on any of my working vacations and a question you may also have to address at some future time: *How deeply should you involve yourself in the internal social, cultural, or economic problems of a host country?*

There are conflicting opinions. Some argue that you are an outsider, a newly arrived non-citizen with no context or history to judge these complex issues; you should say nothing, leaving it to locals to address, debate, and solve. Others maintain that you do not check your morals and values at the customs lounge door, and everyone, citizen and visitor alike, is obliged to speak out against social injustice and immoral and unfair practices wherever and whenever they raise their ugly head. You will, of course, have to

make that difficult decision for yourself based on the specific issues involved while remembering that this decision can have pro-
found consequences on the remainder of your stay. Simply put,
speaking out can cause your working vacation to end a lot earlier
than you expected.

In this case I wanted to share my feelings with those in a position of authority but in a constructive, not confrontational, way,
which I knew would neither be helpful nor appreciated. The Prime
Minister, Dr. Mahathir bin Mohamad, had recently made a major
speech to his party's faithful addressing this very topic, so I thought
it would be a particularly auspicious time to speak out. I approached
the Dean and was told that although he was aware of the problem
there was nothing he could do. (Being Chinese he may have been
afraid of losing his job.) I then decided to try an approach I use back
home when I am steamed up and need to vent—writing a letter to
the editor of the local paper. I crafted a thoughtful, non-threatening
letter to the editor of the *New Straits Times,* the English-language
newspaper that plays a role in Malaysia similar to that of the *New
York Times,* the English-language national newspaper of record. My
wife insisted I let it sit on the computer for a few days before mailing to be sure it was not overly emotional or vitriolic. In a slightly
abridged form it read as follows:

Dear Sirs,

The English expression *tough love* means to care about someone
so much you are willing to tell them things they do not want to
hear but are for their own good. I think the Prime Minister's
recent speech on the problems arising from Malay constitutional privileges was a wonderful example of tough love.

The comments hitting closest to home were those about education, especially the hard work and dedication that are a necessary prerequisite for academic success. This semester I have

the unhappy task of failing almost half of my Malay students. This failure rate has nothing to do with innate ability; instead, it has everything to do with attitude, effort, and commitment. Malay students are lackadaisical about their education. Their absentee rate is 30–40 percent, but when I plead for them to come, I am told they do not like getting up early. I rarely have Malay students come to my office for help, even when they have failed an exam. Worst of all, when Malay students are given a homework project they choose not to do it or take the "low road" and copy the work of others.

It is not hard to explain how to do well—attend class, do the readings, complete the assignments, study for examinations, and seek help if you have difficulty. Most important is the realization that success will not be handed to you. It requires dedication, commitment, and long hours of hard work. I hope that all students will heed these "tough love" words of the Prime Minister.

Sincerely,

Prof. G. Michael Schneider

When I shared the letter with MMU colleagues they congratulated me on my forthright action; their actual words were "You've got balls!" But they laughed at my newcomer's naïveté saying such a controversial article would never be printed in a national newspaper controlled by the Malay-dominated government. Their laughter ended rather abruptly when, three days later, the letter appeared, unedited, at the top of the editorial page under the 24-point banner headline "American Professor Laments Malay Academic Performance."

The following morning I was summoned to the offices of the U.S. Fulbright Commission and castigated for meddling in the internal affairs of a host country. I was told there was a meeting scheduled with government officials and high-level administrators to determine if I should be allowed to remain in my teaching post or be asked to leave the country immediately. While I nervously waited for their verdict, dozens of letters appeared in the *New Straits Times,* many from Malaysian high school teachers and college professors thanking me for addressing a festering problem that was long overdue for an open, honest, and frank debate. One week later I was called into the office of the (Malay) President of MMU and told that he was thoroughly unhappy with my words and, if it were up to him, I would be on the next plane back to the United States. However, he would allow me to remain in my position and finish the semester. His demeanor and body language clearly indicated that this was a decision imposed on him by "higher ups."

My letter opened a floodgate of repressed feelings that spewed forth from all levels of society and all corners of the nation. More letters and articles appeared in the newspaper, and during those remaining days in Malaysia I participated in fractious meetings with students, faculty, and administrators about how to address the serious and complex problem of Malay academic performance vis-à-vis the Chinese and Indian population. Approximately two years after my letter first appeared, I received e-mail from an MMU colleague informing me that Prime Minister Mahathir had just announced that Malay quotas in college and university admissions would end immediately. I am guessing the Prime Minister personally approved publication of my original letter as a "trial balloon" to gauge public feeling about this controversial change. When he read the many positive responses from Malay parents, educators, and school administrators he decided to move forward. I can only assume that if the responses had been angrier and more turbulent the ending to this chapter would have been far less pleasant to write.

I was thankful to be able to complete my term, as there was still much more to see and do. The generous balance remaining in the travel budget opened my eyes to yet another way to stretch this budget even further. Overseas schools and institutions that could not possibly afford the cost of transporting and supporting a long-term visitor from the United States may be able, even eager, to cover the cost of a far less expensive short-term visitor from a neighboring country. Malaysia is surrounded by many interesting Southeast Asian tourist destinations, any one of which makes for an ideal excursion from KL. With that in mind, I contacted the chairs of computer science programs at a half-dozen nearby universities and offered to give public presentations and do curricular consulting in exchange for a single round-trip air ticket from KL and hotel accommodations.

My "local" cold calls were quite successful as three schools responded in the affirmative. This led to our spending four days each, during MMU school holidays, at the Universities of Sarawak and Sabah on the island of Borneo, as well as a six-day visit, during spring break, to Hanoi Technical University in Vietnam, complete with a side trip to Angkor Wat in Cambodia on the return. Since the schools were covering the cost of my air ticket as well as food and lodging, the only hit to my Fulbright travel budget was Ruth's air ticket, and room and board expenses for the time spent in country following completion of my work.

When overseas on a working vacation, be sure to check with schools and institutions in the region to see if they might be interested in hosting a short-term visit. If it works out you will get a trip to an interesting destination, using reserve travel funds to cover spousal costs, while your hosts only have to shell out for a single inexpensive airline ticket from a nearby city, a few nights at a hotel, and a couple of meals. Everyone wins.

Malaysia is a multicultural stewpot of Malay, Chinese, and Indian societies, and someone's religious holiday was always popping up on the school calendar creating a day off here, three days there. Just as Ruth and I celebrated the Hindu festival of *Diwali* in Mauritius, we now participated in the Lion Dance Ceremony of Chinese New Year and the Muslim holiday *Eid ul-Fitr,* a feast celebrating the end of Ramadan. It seemed that each week we were sharing in the rites of some previously unknown religious festival.

The tables were turned on our Malaysian hosts when Ruth and I celebrated Passover that April with Gary Braut, the lone permanent Jewish resident in this bustling city of 1.2 million inhabitants. Gary is a Brooklyn-born orthodox Jew who arrived in KL as a merchant marine seaman and liked it so much he decided to stay. He settled down and set up a successful auto parts business, totally oblivious to the irony of living as an observant Jew in the midst of an overwhelmingly Muslim nation.

Gary held a Passover Seder attended by about forty people only six of whom, Ruth and me included, were Jewish. The other attendees were Muslims, Hindus, and Buddhists whose curiosity was piqued by the advertisement Gary placed in the *New Straits Times* a week earlier announcing, "Passover Seder officiated by an American Rabbi. Dinner included. Everyone welcome." The service was held in his auto parts warehouse, easily identified by the twenty-foot *menorah,* ceremonial candelabra, constructed entirely from used mufflers and tail pipes and prominently displayed by the factory entrance. The food was classic American Passover fare—gefilte fish, matzo ball soup, Mogen David wine, Manischewitz *matzo*—all shipped in from the United States. Observant Muslim women bedecked in colorful *hijabs,* Muslim headscarves, prepared dinner. They may not have been familiar with the customs or the recipes, but the food was nevertheless delicious and tasted just like grandma used to make.

The service leader, Rebbe Velvel, was a yeshiva student from Crown Heights in Brooklyn, flown halfway around the world for just this one evening. (Afterward, he was heading to Surabaya,

Indonesia, to minister to the dozen or so Indonesian Jews living there.) There were *Haggadot,* the story of the Jewish Exodus from Egypt, for everyone including comic book *Haggadot* for children, and the student rabbi did an "explanatory-style" service touching on the history of the Jewish people and the story of the Exodus. Even though Malaysians are used to celebrating the religious holidays of other cultures, they were fascinated by this strange and totally unfamiliar ceremony. They asked lots of questions—"What is that strange writing?" (Hebrew), and "What are those little tassels under the rabbi's shirt?" *(tzitzis).* Following the service they dug into the unfamiliar foods with gusto, one Chinese woman even asking for the recipe for matzoh balls saying it would be an excellent addition to her wonton soup! It was quite a night, and one I remember fondly each year as my family gathers for the Seder in the far more traditional setting of my own dining room.

Although we have participated in the religious festivities of many denominations and cultures, none of them, Passover included, can begin to approach the overpowering sensory experiences of our evening at *Thaipusam,* a Hindu festival celebrating the birth of Lord Subramaniam, youngest son of the God Shiva. The holiday is observed throughout the Hindu world, but nowhere with more exuberance and fervor than Kuala Lumpur, where upwards of one million people attend this annual celebration. It is a memory that is as vivid today as it was that night almost a decade earlier.

The observance lasts for twenty-four hours, but due to the heat and humidity we opted to attend late at night when conditions were a bit less oppressive. Ruth and I boarded a bus in downtown KL at 11:00 p.m. for our trip to the Batu Caves, the festival site, nine miles north of the city center. Because of the immense throng the trip took well over an hour, and we had to get out and walk the last half-mile as the vehicle was unable to navigate the sea of revelers, penitents, and sightseers wending their way to the staging area. The crowds were reminiscent of New York's Times

Square on New Year's Eve. There were food stalls, carnival stands, ear-splitting music, bright lights, and incense—imagine a combination state fair, tent revival meeting, and hard rock mosh pit.

Thaipusam is a holiday when Hindus cleanse themselves of past sins and seek to avoid future adversity via gifts and self-flagellation. On the day of the festival the pilgrims walk nine miles to the festival site, wash themselves in a nearby river, and shave their heads as a sign of repentance. They don a traditional yellow sarong and, using prayers, music, drumming, and repetitive chanting, enter a trance-like state. They become hypnotic, almost catatonic, moving and swaying, pushing and shoving, unconsciously bumping into anyone standing nearby. Once entranced they are pierced with wooden lances, called *vel,* through their tongues, cheeks, and lips, although they do not appear to bleed or feel pain.

The more intense participants have sharp metal hooks pulled through the skin on their backs. These hooks are connected to

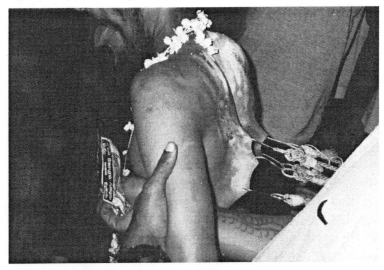

Penetent piercing his flesh at the Hindu Festival of Thaipusam.

ropes to pull a ceremonial chariot, called a *kavadi,* using only their own flesh and muscle. The *kavadi* is decorated with peacock feathers and filled with incense, fruit, milk, honey, and other offerings for Lord Subramaniam. Penitents drag their chariots through the madding crowd shouting and chanting prayers, all the while helped along by friends should they should fall down or faint from exhaustion, ecstasy, or pain. To those unfamiliar with these traditions, watching this mortification of the human body is both fascinating and highly disturbing.

Surrounding the festival grounds are tens of thousands of penitents, hundreds of thousands of helpers/musicians/dancers, and countless sightseers, vendors, and other assorted attendees taking in the multitudinous sounds, sights, and smells of this huge event. In addition to religious activities there is a carnival area along the periphery with stalls selling food and souvenirs, fortune-tellers offering to read your palm, and hawkers selling peacock feathers, sandalwood, and incense.

Temple Cave, the site where pilgrims bring their gifts and receive final absolution, is at the top of a steep hill. An enormous gilded staircase (forty feet wide, 272 steps) snakes up the mountainside, and a seemingly endless procession of supplicants haul their gifts and drag their chariots up the many steps. Tourists are permitted to join the throng, but Ruth and I opted to watch this torchlight parade of pilgrims wind its way up the mountainside, marveling at the impassioned demonstration of religious fervor and human will. We also began plotting our strategy for returning to the parking lot—a nontrivial operation since tens of thousands of pilgrims and visitors were still pouring into the festival site. Fortunately, we found the bus and returned to our apartment at 5:00 a.m. reeking of incense, sandalwood, curry, sweat, and mud. We stood under a hot shower, made a pot of tea, and tried to comprehend all that we had witnessed. Sleep did not arrive until hours later.

For the sake of brevity I will end our Malaysian adventure stories here, omitting our stay in a longhouse with the Iban people of Sarawak, headhunters until the early twentieth century; trekking to view the largest and one of the rarest flower in the world, the giant Rafflesia, a treat for an avid gardener like my wife; lounging on the incomparable beaches of Bali and Langkawi; viewing wild orangutans in the jungles of Borneo; and our visit to Myanmar, once known as Burma, a beautiful but frightening country where every aspect of daily life is monitored and controlled by a brutal military dictatorship. Seven months living and working in

My wife and the giant Rafflesia plant on the island of Borneo.

this fascinating, sometimes frustrating, country provided an unparalleled cultural, intellectual, and professional experience that is truly worth its own book rather than this one brief chapter. Where Mauritius was a pleasant, relaxing, and totally serene tropical sabbatical, Malaysia could not have been more different—a nonstop hubbub of exotic travel, cultural immersion, sensory overload, and social and political controversy. The wonderful thing is that both these disparate types of working vacations were enormously rewarding and thoroughly enjoyable.

When we returned to the United States in late July, Ruth and I knew with certainty that we wanted to duplicate these experiences yet one more time. After all, if we could enjoy three wonderful cold-call working vacations (Kenya, Turkey, Zimbabwe) why not three exhilarating Fulbrights? Unfortunately, Rule 624.2 of the Fulbright rulebook states quite adamantly "the maximum number of traditional Fulbright awards for Senior Scholars is limited to two." That's a pretty clear statement. It would seem I had run out of luck and my Fulbright well had officially run dry. Or had it?

CHAPTER 11

Climb Any Mountain

I was the fortunate recipient of two Fulbright grants, a highly competitive award most professionals would be pleased to receive even once. I would have liked to try for a "three-peat," but the rules were unambiguous—a maximum of two. No exceptions. No loopholes. This fount of no-cost travel, mined so successfully the last few years, was now officially tapped out.

In fall 2002, about sixteen months after returning from Malaysia, I received an unsolicited e-mail from CIES, the Council for the International Exchange of Scholars, alerting me to an overseas exchange program recently authorized by the U.S. State Department. Because I was the recipient of an earlier federal grant I had automatically been added to their e-mail contact list, a fortunate circumstance as I am not sure when, left to my own devices, I would have unearthed information about this new opportunity. That was a good lesson to learn and now, whenever I fill out an application or complete the terms of a work contract, I check to see if there is a mailing list for automatic notification of future openings and new initiatives. Four years after my posting in Nepal I still receive and happily devour the *United States Educational Foundation in Nepal Newsletter,* the primary source of information about college and university employment opportunities in that country.

The new educational exchange grant is the Senior Specialist program, and it was created to solve a problem bedeviling the Fulbright office for years—their difficulty filling positions in certain critical high-demand areas. Many international institutions were finding it hard, if not impossible, to attract visitors in law, medicine, science, and business because skilled professionals in these areas are often unable to leave their positions and travel overseas for three to nine months. As an academic it is not too difficult to get away for three months during summer break or apply for and receive a six- or nine-month sabbatical. Surgeons, litigators, research directors, software designers, CEOs, and the like may not have that degree of flexibility. In addition, completing the Fulbright application form can take days, days that busy people often do not have. The result of these impediments was that CIES was receiving scores of applications from professors in the humanities, fine arts, and social sciences, but far fewer from physical scientists, health specialists, business professionals, and skilled workers outside of academia.

Their solution was to create a new grant program with leaves lasting just two to six weeks, a duration that should be accessible to even the most time-strapped professional. Detailed information on these grants is available at www.cies.org/specialists/. While it would be impossible to teach a semester-length course or carry out long-term research in this brief period, it is certainly feasible to give talks, present workshops, and do consulting, all potentially useful activities to an overseas institution.

The Fulbright office went even further. To reduce the time required to complete the application, they placed the onus of obtaining a Senior Specialist grant on the host institution rather than the applicant. A Senior Specialist candidate completes a relatively short biographical form that is reviewed by a panel of experts at the State Department. If you pass this review and are deemed qualified your name and résumé are placed on the U.S. State Department *Senior Specialist Roster,* a listing of skilled professionals ordered by area of specialization. That's it. Once your name is ensconced on that roster, where it remains for five years, you can sit back, relax, and wait for the phone to ring.

It is the overseas institution—school, hospital, library, research center—that must complete all the remaining steps. They determine what type of professional they wish to invite, review the roster of available specialists, select the single most qualified individual to meet their needs, and contact the U.S. Embassy or Fulbright Commission to inform them of their choice and finish the application process. Final approval for a visit is made by the State Department which, if the request is approved, will call with the news that you have been selected for an all-expenses paid two- to six-week working vacation—just the kind of unexpected, out-of-the-blue call I love to receive. If the destination is unattractive or the proposed dates are inconvenient the recipient is free to reject the invitation without penalty and without jeopardizing his or her chances for future invitations. Best of all, the rules explicitly state it is permissible receive a Senior Specialist grant *in addition to* any other awards you may have received in the past. This changed everything, and that apparently dry Fulbright well had suddenly resumed flowing. I was back in business.[9]

I filled out the application form, was vetted and approved by the State Department, and added to the growing on-line roster of qualified specialists. I then sat back waiting to hear from Washington, ready to pack at a moment's notice and head out to the

---

9. The rules on Fulbright grants were modified in 2007. Now a candidate may receive a maximum of *two* Fulbright grants of any type, Scholar or Senior Specialist.

airport, but a year later still no offer, still no invitation. The situation was becoming uncomfortably similar to the conditions described at the beginning of Chapter 3, where I was waiting for someone to call with the offer of an all-expense paid working vacation to some exotic locale, an offer that never materialized.

Even though the decades and the miles had turned me into a savvy and sophisticated world traveler, I had forgotten a fundamental principle first learned more than twenty years ago: *It is almost always a losing proposition to sit back and wait for something good to happen to you by chance. Instead, you must proactively and aggressively campaign to make those good things happen.* Someone on the specialist roster was going to get an invitation, but unless I did something on behalf of my own candidacy there was only a slim chance that someone would be me.

In the past year, while waiting for that call from Washington I had tried, unsuccessfully, to obtain a short-term teaching position at the Royal University of Bhutan—a forlorn quest recounted in Chapter 7. This failure, however, did nothing to diminish my desire to live and work in South Asia, so I decided to try to locate a working vacation in Nepal, an equally beautiful Himalayan kingdom immediately to the west of Bhutan.[10] I scanned the Web for information on schools in Nepal that could use someone with my skills and discovered the home page of Kathmandu University or KU, as it is commonly known. This is a relatively new school, founded in 1991, with an emphasis on technical education including programs in engineering, mathematics, and information technology—just my cup of tea.

I sent an unsolicited e-mail to the chair of the KU Computer

---

10. At that time I could not apply for a Fulbright to Bhutan as they do not have either a Fulbright Commission or a U.S. Embassy, making them ineligible. However, that rule was changed and the first Fulbrighter to Bhutan was posted to the country in 2009.

Science Department, the cold call reborn, asking if they might like to host a visiting professor of computer science for six weeks during summer 2004. My inquiry, however, was quite different in tone from those earlier calls to Kenya, Turkey, and Zimbabwe because this time I was asking them only to host me, not pay for me—a far easier sell. In that e-mail I described my background, experience, skills, and previous work at Multimedia University in Malaysia, also a new Asian school specializing in technical education. I listed the professional activities I could offer during a visit, such as curriculum evaluation, faculty workshops, and public talks. Finally, I reminded them once again that my visit would be at *no cost to them*, emphasis included, and outlined the steps they needed to follow to complete the Senior Specialist application, including exactly where to get an application form and where on the form to write in my name as the person they wished to invite.

Right about now you might be wondering if I am overstepping some ethical or moral boundary. After all, the intent of this new grant is for the host country, not the applicant, to select and invite the most qualified person for their open position. Was this aggressive action in selling myself violating some unwritten rule of conduct?

Absolutely not, and sending unsolicited letters to prospective institutions is completely kosher. It is no different from what happens when a new store opens. A smart owner does not sit back and wait for customers to walk in the front door. Instead, he or she advertises the high-quality merchandise, low prices, and personal service, and invites everyone to stop in for a visit. I did exactly the same thing but on a more individual level—advertising my skills and experience and inviting the faculty of KU to "give me a try." It was still their decision either to go forward with the process or throw my e-mail into the trash. My advertising campaign worked, spectacularly so, as less than three months after sending that e-mail I received a call from CIES informing me that—surprise, surprise—I had been invited by Kathmandu University to be a Senior Specialist in computer science for six weeks the following summer.

The moral of this story is simple: Don't be modest or reserved when it comes to jumping into the scrum and fighting for that working vacation. Make the fullest and most vigorous use of every opportunity that crosses your path. If someone gives you the name of a contact, use it, being sure to fully catalog all the helpful professional services you can offer. When you read about an overseas possibility, send e-mail emphasizing your many strengths and skills. If an attractive new funding program opens up, apply for it explaining why you are by far the best-qualified candidate for the posting. Not exactly nuclear physics, but it is surprising and sad how often people hear about a great overseas opportunity, think that it is something they might love to try, and then do absolutely nothing—the working-vacation equivalent of "Let's do lunch."

As a dramatic example of even more aggressive action than my simple e-mail, an academic acquaintance recently posted a message on Facebook announcing to the entire world that "Professor X is seeking a Senior Specialist invitation for four to six weeks during the upcoming summer," then going on to describe his research achievements, academic skills and classroom experience in great detail. Facebook, for goodness sake! Some might scoff at his *chutzpah* in seeking a prestigious academic award using the electronic equivalent of a grocery store bulletin board, but I think it is brilliant and may even borrow his idea in the near future. Regardless of what you may personally think about his tactics, the truth is that Professor X is far more likely to be the successful recipient of a Senior Specialist grant than those of you doing nothing but sitting home waiting for a call from Washington.

So on May 20, 2004, Ruth and I journeyed to the airport for yet another agonizingly long flight, this time from Minneapolis to Kathmandu via Osaka and New Delhi. We arrived two days later and were met at the airport by staff of the American Center, the branch of the U.S. Embassy responsible for visiting American students and scholars in Nepal. (It functions much like the Fulbright Commission in Malaysia.) They drove us to our home for the next six weeks, a residence that turned out to be a totally unexpected, but most pleasant, surprise.

The front gates of the grounds swung open to reveal, in the middle of this poor Asian nation, a lovely four-bedroom French colonial home built in a style reminiscent of New Orleans, complete with balcony and ornate wrought iron latticework. This magnificent edifice sat on three acres of manicured gardens, both floral and edible, and included four servants: a watchman; maid; gardener; and Ram, the cook, server, shopper, and all-around household manager who could clarify for us, in impeccable English, any aspect of Nepalese culture or society that confused or befuddled.

This magnificent home is owned by Ms. Olga Murray, founder of the Nepalese Youth Foundation, http://www.nepalyouth foundation.org/index.html, a U.S.-based charity offering education, housing, and medical care to poor Nepalese girls who would otherwise be conscripted into a life of prostitution or forced child labor. For three months each year Olga returns to the United States to raise funds for her foundation. During her absence she is happy to have people live in her house so the staff can continue to work and receive a paycheck. (We were responsible for their salary during our stay.)

I had written the director of the American Center months before our arrival informing him that we would be extremely interested in renting a nice home in the city should something become available. KU is located in the tiny hamlet of Dhulikhel, about twenty-three miles outside the city, but Ruth and I wanted to live in Kathmandu and commute as I had done in Malaysia. Since I contacted the director about rental housing before anyone else, I was first in line and ended up with what surely must be the finest temporary accommodations in the country—yet another example of the benefits of early, decisive action when planning a working vacation.

While we were marveling at our good fortune, Ram called us to lunch, served *al fresco* on the patio in the midst of a garden perfumed with the scent of roses and flowering jacaranda trees. As we love all types of Asian cuisine we were eager to see what he prepared for our first meal in Nepal only to discover that it was, of all things, tuna noodle casserole. Ruth and I had traveled ten thousand miles to the far side of the globe, only to be served a meal more appropriate for a Minnesota potluck dinner. After getting over our initial shock we learned the previous resident of the house was a professor from the University of Iowa who was, to put it mildly, not very adventurous at the dinner table. Our unexpected luncheon was the result of Ram's assumption that, as fellow Midwesterners, we would have similar dietary inclinations. Fearing our next meal might be mac and cheese or breaded fish sticks, we quickly convinced him of our love for spicy Nepalese and Indian cuisine, and for the next six weeks dined magnificently, often on fruits and vegetables grown right outside our bedroom balcony.

To navigate the twenty-three miles to work I decided to rent a car, disregarding the pleadings and warnings of Embassy personnel. I wanted the freedom a car brings and assumed it would be an easy drive since both Kathmandu and Dhulikhel are situated on the Arneko Highway, the country's main east-west road link. I soon discovered that this lifeline of commerce and transportation was smaller than the side street in front of my home and nowhere near as well maintained. Even worse, the local drivers made New York cabbies appear courteous and well behaved. The cardinal rule of driving in Nepal is "Don't blink!" Passing on curves and driving on the sidewalk don't even rate a second mention in the litany of traffic sins, while cows meandering across the road are not an uncommon sight. Turning, passing, stopping, and merging are all preceded by prolonged honking so you can imagine the non-stop cacophony surrounding you at all times. As for traffic infrastructure such as lane markers—you must be kidding; stop signs—in your dreams; traffic lights—when the messiah comes. In Nepal the most important "infrastructures" are steely nerves, a death grip on the wheel, and a good strong bumper for when the first two are not enough.

This craziness is made worse by the range of vehicles using the road. The Arneko Highway hosts a crazy quilt of cars, trucks, buses, motorcycles, mopeds, bicycles, pedestrians, donkey carts, cows, and lawnmowers. That last one confused me since I didn't think gardening was a major concern of most residents. It turns out that in Nepal, used Chinese riding lawnmowers are cheaper than mopeds and, as long as you don't mind ambling along at a leisurely 5–10 mph, an inexpensive form of motorized transport. I was also warned that Nepalese police assume all foreign visitors are rich and able to bear the full cost of an accident so instead of a "no fault" model for auto insurance they use a "your fault" model, not a very comforting thought.

Even though I had successfully motored thousands of miles across Morocco, Mauritius, and Malaysia without problem or accident, I reluctantly accepted the fact that there are indeed limitations to my love of "adventure tourism" and my tolerance for risk of great bodily harm. I returned the rental car the following day as embassy employees gave me that smirking "I told you so" look. For the remainder of the stay I took a bus to school, content to let others deal with the bumper-car mentality of Nepalese drivers.

Ruth also had to deal with this traffic chaos as she volunteered two days a week at an elementary school for the children of *dalits,* or untouchables, the lowest social caste. Since the school was ten miles away she accepted the offer of transportation from a teacher living in our neighborhood—on his motorcycle. With helmet firmly attached and a boa constrictor-like grip around the driver's mid-section, the two of them navigated in and through that same motley collection of vehicles.

Ruth helped students with their English skills and offered lessons in American history, literature, and culture. Although Nepal has officially outlawed discrimination based on caste since 1962, *dalits* often attend their own schools so as not to face the constant humiliation and harassment directed at them by children of higher caste families. Although their parents have been relegated to the bottom rung of the social ladder, the children were bright, curious, and eager to learn, while the school was modern, well supplied, and staffed by enthusiastic faculty. It was quite the opposite of what you might envision from a school for society's have-nots and the antithesis of many poor, inner city American institutions where anger, frustration, and despair often run rampant.

Even though we were in Nepal for only six weeks, Ruth was able to participate in this rewarding volunteer opportunity. No matter how brief your visit, the non-working spouse should always be able to find ways to stay intellectually occupied and be able to contribute to the host country. One of the best ways to locate a volunteer opportunity is to contact the U.S. Embassy about a month before arrival, describing your background and letting them know you are interested in part-time volunteer work. They will usually be happy to do the legwork needed to find a good match for your abilities.

In spite of its extreme poverty—Nepal is the second poorest country outside the African continent and the fifteenth poorest in the world—Kathmandu University, located in the Himalayan foothills, is an excellent, well-funded school. The faculty hold advanced degrees from fine Indian universities; are highly knowledgeable, skilled classroom instructors; and are current with new developments. They were also extremely gracious hosts, including us in many of their social activities both during and after school. For example, each day at noon they would collect me from my office and take me to lunch at the school cafeteria. On the first day, believing (like Ram) that I might not be able to handle the spiciness of Nepalese food, they arranged for the cafeteria to prepare a cheeseburger for me only to discover I would have much preferred the *thukpa,* Nepalese vegetable-noodle stew, they were slurping down with gusto. Fortunately, I was able to quickly correct their misunderstanding and no further cheeseburgers came off the grill.

The pace of life on a Specialist grant was more hectic then we were used to. Having only six weeks in country, not six months, we would solicit friends, colleagues, and neighbors for suggestions on places to go and things to do. Then, heeding their advice, we would fill our evenings, weekends, and holidays with visits to suggested sites. On shorter working vacations, when you may not have sufficient time on your own to leisurely uncover out-of-the-way gems and off-the-beaten-path treasures, the best advice I can give is *trust the locals.* The Lonely Planet, Frommer's, and Fodor's are just fine for identifying the best known and most popular tourist sights, but it is friends and neighbors who can help you discover those less well-known destinations that can make a stay truly memorable.

One of our more unusual destinations, to say the least, was Dakshinkali, a Hindu temple set in a picturesque river valley twelve miles south of the city, but it is certainly not a visit for either the squeamish or card-carrying members of the SPCA—Society for the Prevention of Cruelty to Animals. The temple is dedicated to Kali, the "Black Goddess" of death and destruction who, tradition says, can only be appeased by the warm blood of a freshly killed animal. Until two hundred years ago that "animal" was often a lower caste *dalit,* but in 1780 Nepal outlawed human sacrifice so Kali must now be appeased by the blood of goats, lambs, roosters, and ducks.

Every Saturday morning scores of worshippers come to Dakshinkali carrying their live cargo. They proceed to the sacrificial altar adorned with Hindu religious symbols—snakes, monkeys, tridents, garudas (mythological bird-like creatures)—as well as dozens of statues, large and small, of the goddess Kali. On a typical Saturday it is not unusual to see thousands of people dragging their wriggling offerings while hundreds more watch and feed off these activities—souvenir hawkers, goat and rooster sellers, *sadhus* (Hindu holy men) asking for alms, lepers begging for scraps, soldiers keeping order, and the infrequent Western tourist.

At the altar a holy man helps the worshipper's family complete the ceremony, which involves prayers and gifts of flowers, fruits, or rice. The sacrificial animal is then handed to one of the professional butchers who, in the open for all to see, takes a razor-sharp knife and slices off its head. For larger animals like goats this often cannot be accomplished with a single stroke, and one can only imagine the suffering these poor animals endure. The butcher aims the stream of blood pulsating from the severed arteries at one of the statues of Kali, dousing it completely and any tourist who, in quest of that perfect photograph, wanders too close to the action.

The holy man keeps the animal head as a gift while the decapitated body is returned to the penitent. It is only the blood sacrifice that Kali asks for, so the family is free to feast upon the remains. Often, this turns into a festive barbecue in which the animal is cooked over a campfire by the side of the adjacent river. The contrast between children playing and families laughing and eating, while a short distance away there is copious and painful bloodletting, is hard for a non-Hindu to understand or even watch.

Not all our Nepalese adventures were quite so grisly. Midway through our stay, during a three-day school holiday, we flew Yeti Airlines (honestly) to the Himalayan village of Lukla, landing on a tiny runway carved from the side of a snow-capped mountain. At one end of the tarmac sits a steep half-mile drop-off while the other side terminates in a sheer rock wall; neither one is a sight to

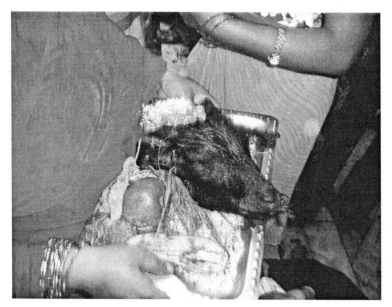

Animal head gift for the Goddess Kali.

inspire confidence during landing. To help arriving planes come to a stop before running abruptly into that rock wall, the pavement is canted upward at a stomach-wrenching 12 percent, the steepest runway incline in the world. On departure the downslope helps planes reach take-off velocity before careening into the half-mile-deep abyss.[11]

Although you might think this would scare away all but the most foolhardy of travelers, Lukla is actually one of the busiest airports in the country as it is where most climbers start their trek to Mt. Everest. We were met at the airport by a Sherpa porter who carried our gear and guided us along the Everest Trail, the same

---

11. The Discovery Channel ran a TV show entitled "Extreme Airports" that rated Lukla, Nepal as the most dangerous and most frightening airport in the world. Glad we did not see it before deciding to make the trip.

trail used by Sherpa Tenzing Norgay and Sir Edmund Hillary in their 1953 conquest of the mountain. Because of limited time, not to mention limited lung capacity, we hiked to the small mountain hamlet of Phakding, only about a quarter of the way to base camp but still a trek of unparalleled grandeur. Chomolungma, as Everest is known to locals, was socked in by clouds and not visible from the trail (more about that later), but there was still enough spectacular Himalayan scenery on display to make this the most resplendent trek Ruth and I have experienced. I was feeling rather pleased, even cocky, about my ability to handle the 10,000 foot altitude until I was abruptly passed by a Sherpa porter far older than I, wearing old sneakers and toting a 130 pound load strapped to his forehead, destined for the marketplace at Namche Bazaar, 3,000 feet higher and a day's hike away.

We spent that night at a B&B in Phakding listening to stories, translated into English by our guide, about life in this remote Khumbu region of eastern Nepal during the seven months of the year when the trail is not chockablock full of trekkers, daytrippers, and Japanese tour groups. We ate a superb Nepalese meal of *momos*, Nepali meat dumplings; cauliflower curry; and *dal bhat*, rice with lentils, prepared by the owner's wife and daughter. For dessert we had, of all things, apple strudel. I thought this must be yet another concession to our supposedly tame Western palates, only to see it on the menu of virtually every restaurant, hotel, kiosk, and hut along the trail.

Many years ago, Swiss and Austrian climbers came to Nepal to try their hand at peaks higher than those in their homeland, and they brought with them not only their mountaineering skills but also their taste in food. They introduced strudel to the locals who loved it, planted apple trees along the steep hillsides, and adopted this classic European dish as their own, just as Americans have done with pizza, tacos, and chop suey. I enjoyed a second helping of this cross-cultural sweet before heading off to bed. The next

Sherpa porter carrying over 100 lbs. of gear with his forehead.

day Ruth and I trekked back to Lukla and returned home, cling-ing tightly to each other during take-off until we were confident the plane would become airborne before reaching that 3,000 foot vertical plunge looming directly in front of our eyes.

Those six weeks flew by quickly and all too soon we found our-selves at a downtown Kathmandu restaurant enjoying a lovely going-away dinner in our honor sponsored by my computer sci-ence colleagues. While I still believe that four to six months is the ideal duration for a working vacation, when that amount of time is neither available nor an option, living and working overseas for four to six weeks can still be a rewarding and intellectually stimulating experience. It certainly should not be dismissed out of hand as too brief to provide any meaningful cultural immersion. Besides, if you have additional time and desire a longer stay simply add a side trip to your itinerary when the working vacation component is finished, exactly what Ruth and I did.

Since the financial terms of a Specialist grant are, like the Fulbright Scholar award, quite generous, there was enough money remaining in the account to cover the cost of a seven-day overland journey to Tibet. We made travel arrangements in town and, following my last day at work, boarded a bus in Kathmandu for the five-hour trip to the border. We walked across the Hangmu Bridge into Tibet and met our rental Jeep and driver for the four-day, six-hundred-mile drive to the Tibetan capital of Lhasa.

The Friendship Highway, as the road is known, must surely be the most scenic, not to mention frightening road in the world, passing within viewing distance of more than a dozen of the highest peaks in the world, all over 25,000 feet. We passed the turn-off to the Everest base camp, Tibetan side, only twenty miles away, but once again it was socked in by clouds and not visible from the road (more about that still later). Luckily, every other major peak was clearly visible against the bright blue sky, creating a panorama of unmatched beauty—as witnessed by the cover photograph taken during the drive. The road is mostly unpaved, unmarked, and unfenced, and there were times when the wheels came within inches of a sheer cliff. Our Chinese driver spoke hardly any English, the one exception being the phrase "OK, no problem," usually uttered immediately after navigating a particularly scary section of highway. However, his language limitations—actually ours, as we were in his country—did not matter at all as the views from the Jeep's windows were more than enough for us in the way of travel narration.

The Friendship Highway is the second highest motorable road in the world, climbing from the Nepal border to the Gyatsola Pass at an altitude of 5,220 meters or 17,125 feet.[12] This is a mile and a half higher than our trek along the Everest trail and even slightly higher than the Everest base camp. It is hard for anyone who is not an experienced mountaineer to imagine the difficulty of even the most minor physical activity at this altitude. It took all my focused mental efforts to take a stroll around the markers, memorials, and souvenir sellers that ringed the pass. I dropped a coin and the simple act of bending down and picking it up necessitated my stopping to rest. Neither Ruth nor I succumbed to altitude sickness, a very real and serious problem at this height, but we could barely summon the effort to tell each other how much fun we were having.

One of the best things about the drive from Kathmandu to Lhasa is that it traverses numerous small towns and villages fighting to maintain their indigenous Tibetan Buddhist culture. Those four days and nights along the Friendship Highway visiting traditional homes, markets, and monasteries, were the highlight of the trip, especially after arriving in the capital of Lhasa and seeing what has occurred there in the last few years. This once remote mountain hideaway, believed to be the inspiration for the fictional utopian valley of Shangri-La, now looks and feels much like any other provincial Chinese capital.

The Han Chinese community now represents a majority of the population, and most stores and shops are owned by Chinese merchants selling "authentic Tibetan handicrafts" made in Guangzhou, Dalian, or Hong Kong. The only Buddhist schools and monasteries remaining open are those helping to maintain and grow the lucrative Western tourist trade. Even the Potala, the 999-room ancestral home of the Dalai Lama and the iconic embodiment of this

---

12. The highest road in the world passes through the Khardung Pass in Kashmir, India at an altitude of 5,359 meters, about 17,582 feet. This is only 450 feet higher than the Friendship Highway at Gyatsola.

mountain kingdom, has been converted to a museum and is mostly empty. Our time in Lhasa was somewhat of a disappointment, but it was more than made up for by those magical four days along the road.

We flew back to Kathmandu to reclaim our belongings from storage, say goodbye to the household staff, and return to Minneapolis. About an hour into the short two-hour flight the pilot came on the public address system to announce that passengers on the right side of the aircraft should look out their window to catch a view of Mt. Everest. I turned around and there it was. When we tried to see it earlier, first from the Everest trail and then from the Friendship Highway, we had been on the ground looking up, unable to see anything because of thick cloud cover. Now, however, we were flying far above the clouds and able to enjoy a beautiful, unobstructed view of the highest mountain in the world. It had taken three attempts, but on our last day in Nepal we finally saw Mt. Everest. I couldn't have scripted a better ending.

We finally see Mt. Everest on the return flight to Kathmandu.

CHAPTER 12

The Great Khan

My school, Macalester College, is blessed with a multitude of superb teacher/scholars—a National Book Award winner, an Antarctic explorer with a mountain named after him, and even a Hollywood screenwriter. In the midst of all these stars sits an academic supernova, Prof. Jack Weatherford, an anthropologist and best-selling author who has written extensively about Native Americans, including *Indian Givers* (1988), *Native Roots* (1991), and *Savages and Civilization* (1994). For the last fifteen years Jack has focused his scholarship on Mongolia and its founder, Genghis Khan, culminating in the award-winning book *Genghis Khan and the Making of the Modern World* (2004). He is a frequent guest on radio and television discussing the great Khan's contributions to modern society, and in 2007 the President of Mongolia awarded him the Order of the Polar Star, his nation's highest civilian honor.

One of the pleasures of being at a small liberal arts college like Macalester is the frequent cross-pollination of disciplines, and I would often enjoy lunch or afternoon coffee with an eclectic mix of colleagues in fields far removed from my own—economics, philosophy, art, physics, and anthropology. It was fall 2005 and Prof. Weatherford had just returned from an extended stay at Genghis Khan University in Ulan Bator, Mongolia's capitol, where its president, Lkhagvasuren (Mongolians often use a single name), asked him to see if any other Macalester faculty might wish to visit the school in a professional capacity. Jack knew I enjoyed living and working overseas, often joking that I was a frustrated cultural anthropologist trapped within a computer scientist's body. Over a leisurely lunch at the Campus Center, he related details of this work opportunity while cautioning that the school was poor and could provide little in the way of financial assistance.

I have argued repeatedly that you should pursue any working vacation prospect that unexpectedly appears on the horizon, and suddenly this unique and totally unanticipated possibility had landed, without warning, in my very own lap. Here was a school desirous of bringing in short-term visitors, although it cannot afford to pay them, and a U.S. State Department eager to provide funding, via the Senior Specialist program, for just these types of short-term professional visits—a fortuitous conjunction of two travel opportunities.

Our previous working vacations had all been to countries that my wife and I had discussed thoroughly, studied extensively, and consciously selected as places we would like to live and work. This situation was quite different. Neither of us had ever considered Mongolia as a potential destination, and we knew nothing at all about the country other than the stories Jack would regale us with during those shared meals. It was certainly not on my top-ten list of places to see before I die. However, when planning a working vacation a helpful guideline to keep in mind is *don't be afraid of destinations you have never considered and which you currently know nothing about.*

Unplanned opportunities don't always coordinate well with your personal likes and dislikes. They don't anticipate and accommodate your specific desires and dreams. Instead, they have the nasty habit of popping up at unexpected times with offers to unfamiliar places: countries we may not think about except when watching their colorfully dressed Olympic athletes marching into some far-off stadium. As long as these countries are safe, stable, and friendly, which Mongolia certainly is, investigate them fully and give them serious consideration as they could provide a fascinating, not to mention no-cost, cultural adventure.

Another benefit of travel to an unexpected destination is that although it may not be a place you had planned to go, it may be *near* someplace you had planned to go, as was the case with us. Ever since our ill-timed 1989 trip to China was cancelled because of the massacres in Tiananmen Square, we had tried unsuccessfully to plan a return. Now we had that chance. Ruth and I decided to try for a Senior Specialist grant to Genghis Khan University with a long, leisurely stopover in China, Mongolia's neighbor to the south, added to the itinerary compliments of Uncle Sam.

Since it is the host institution, not the guest, that initiates a Senior Specialist request, I first had to motivate the leadership of Genghis Khan University to complete the grant application, being sure to name me as their preferred visitor. That was not a problem. After receiving my e-mail that included the key phrase "a good friend of Prof. Jack Weatherford," the wheels of Mongolian bureaucracy shifted smoothly into high gear. After only a few months I received that eagerly anticipated call from Washington informing me I had been formally requested as a Senior Specialist in computer science for a five-week visit to Mongolia during summer 2006, a request I quickly accepted. Why they reduced the proposed visit from six weeks to five will forever remain a mystery. Perhaps State Department budgets were tight.

The obvious moral of this story is, to paraphrase Sir Isaac Newton, when applying for a working vacation it is helpful to stand of the shoulders of a giant. If you know someone with a close connection to an overseas institution be sure to ask if you may use him or her as a professional reference. Dropping a familiar, well-respected name into a personal communication can greatly smooth the path to success—just as Paul Tymann and Jon Pearce had used my name a few years earlier to help them obtain positions in Zimbabwe and Turkey, respectively.

On May 20, 2006, Ruth and I departed Minneapolis for Ulan Bator, Mongolia with a fourteen-day stopover in China, a cost I was able to cover with funds from my Senior Specialist stipend. We did not pre-book any internal flights or tours other than our initial three-nights lodging at a Beijing hotel; we did not want to arrive after an exhausting twelve-hour flight only to start looking for a place to sleep. We spent a few days getting over jet lag and enjoying the sights of Beijing before visiting a nearby office of CTS, China Travel Service, the official tourism and travel agency of the People's Republic. The staff, who all spoke excellent English, helped us plan our continuing travels throughout China and book hotels, flights to Xi'an and Chongqing, and a boat tour through the Three Gorges region of Szechwan Province, all at prices a fraction of what they would be if purchased in the United States.

I know that some travelers are nervous arriving in a foreign country without a fully booked, confirmed, and reconfirmed hour-by-hour travel schedule. While a carefully planned itinerary may be reassuring, it can also be a costly and unnecessary luxury, especially in a country with a vibrant and competitive tourism industry eager to assist overseas visitors. It has been our experience that you often do better waiting until you arrive and visiting a local travel agent to purchase accommodations, transportation, and tours.[13] Not only will you likely save a good deal of money, but you do not have to plan the entire itinerary in advance. For example, we initially thought we might spend five or six days in Beijing, but after three days we were ready to move on. Similarly, we had originally planned to fly from Beijing to Shanghai, but after discussions with our hotel concierge and the travel agency we changed those plans to include a scenic four-day boat trip on the Yangtze.

By not planning the entire stay you maintain the flexibility not only to determine the location and duration of stops along the way but also to change those stops based on helpful information gleaned after arrival. This type of unscripted, spontaneous travel is similar to what we did when we bummed around the United States or Europe in our youth. At that time we would never have a rigid, day-by-day schedule of planned activities and would certainly not fret over its absence. Instead, we let the evening and next day's plans be serendipitously determined by what happened and whom we met that morning or afternoon. It works for teens and twenties, and it can work quite well for thirty-somethings and beyond.

We spent eleven days traveling and eating our way around China, including not only the "biggies" of Chinese tourism—the Great Wall, Forbidden City, Terra Cotta Warriors—but also some less well-known sights, such as the city of Chongqing, the "Pepper Capital of China," where we dined on *huǒ guō*, the famous, or perhaps I should say infamous, Szechwan Spicy Hot Pot. We read about this local delicacy in a guidebook and decided to visit one of the many well-known *huǒ guō* restaurants in the city. When we

---

13. The one exception to this advice is when a country or a region offers special reduced-price transportation or sightseeing deals such as the Eurail Pass or the Japanese JR Rail Pass available only to tourists. Frequently these special tourist passes must be purchased outside the country prior to arrival.

placed our order by pointing to a picture on the menu the waiter, who spoke no English, shook his head to indicate "no" and put his hands around his throat in a gesture that seemed to say if we ate this we would surely die. Since I would not be deterred by his pantomimed warning, he fetched a customer who spoke a little English, enough to say "too hot–don't want," but I stubbornly replied, "Yes, this is exactly what I want." Eventually the waiter got the idea and grudgingly trundled off to fill our request.

Ruth and I laughed knowing we loved hot food and were seasoned veterans of the spiciest Thai and Sri Lankan restaurants back home. Well, that cockiness quickly disappeared with the arrival of our order. Yes, we could see chicken and mushrooms floating around the pot, but they were hard to separate from the fiery red Szechwan peppers cascading from the steaming broth like a volcano spewing lava. We took a spoonful and began to sweat profusely as other customers in the restaurant looked on in amusement. We could not possibly eat the dish as it was so we decided to pick out the peppers, hoping to reduce its intensity to something more palatable. Fifteen minutes of adroit chopstick manipulations produced a fiery pile almost six inches across.

Sadly, though, these efforts to tame our entree were to no avail. The heat level had not decreased and, in fact, had grown even more intense. While we were busy chasing down peppers with our chopsticks, the goodies were stewing in the peppery broth becoming even more potent than when they first arrived. After a few more cautious sips we gave up, paid the bill, and prepared to leave. We thought the cooks may have been playing a practical joke, but as we headed to the exit a perusal of hot pots on other tables showed they looked exactly like ours—all laden with enough fiery red peppers to generate sweating and panting from the aroma alone. After this experience I decided I would have the volume of my next authentic Szechwan meal turned down a few notches. I also decided that in the future, when venturing into unexplored culinary territory, it would be wise to adopt a policy of listening to the locals, as they often know best.

After a glorious two weeks enjoying the heartland of China we returned to Beijing to catch a flight to Ulan Bator, or UB as it is called, a short trip in time but a massive journey in terms of modernity, wealth, power, and people. While the population of China exceeds 1.3 billion, Mongolia is home to only 2.3 million, less than the Minneapolis/St. Paul metropolitan area. The country is vast, encompassing over six hundred thousand square miles, more than twice the size of Texas, making it the most sparsely populated inhabited country on Earth. And, while China is an economic superpower sprouting glass and steel skyscrapers while racing headlong into the twenty-first century, Mongolia is a trip back in time to simpler days when nomadic families lived in *yurts*; herded yaks, goats, sheep, and camels; and moved with the change of seasons. The distance from Beijing to Ulan Bator should really not be measured in miles but in centuries.

We were met at the airport by Lkhagvasuren, his wife Chujilmah, and Muki, an English teacher from Genghis Khan University who functioned as both greeter and translator since the president and his wife spoke little English. We were taken to our apartment, a clean, comfortable, Western-style one-bedroom within walking distance of the school, and given a couple of days to recover from jet lag before reporting for work—they assumed we had flown to Mongolia from Minnesota without a layover.

We decided to use our first few days to investigate this burgeoning city now home to 40 percent of the population. To accomplish this I first had to learn four words of Mongolian, the only words I mastered during the stay—and, no, they are not "Where is the bathroom?" or "Two more beers, please." Not a single taxi driver flagged down on the streets of UB spoke or understood a word of English, while I was never able to conquer the strange, guttural sounds of Mongolian well enough to be understood whenever I attempted to pronounce the name of a multi-syllabic destination. As a survival tactic I learned to say the four simple words *zum* (right), *baroon* (left), *chigere* (straight ahead), and *stoltz* (stop) and used them, along with hand gestures and a city map, to direct our driver as he weaved in and out of traffic. If I was not sure exactly where I was going, I would point the vehicle in the proper direction, drive for a while, and get out, hoping we were within walking distance of our goal. Since a typical in-town cab fare ran about 50¢, it really didn't matter if I was wrong as we would simply hop in the next cab that came by and try again, eventually converging on the desired destination.

Unfortunately, what we discovered in those first few days was that Ulan Bator is neither a very interesting nor a very pretty city. It holds little in the way of historical significance since it did not become a major urban area until well into the twentieth century—in 1910 its population was less than 25,000. It has little architectural grandeur since the majority of buildings in the city center were constructed after World War II in the foreboding Soviet cinder-block style reminiscent of the depressing high-tech cities that litter the Siberian plains. Paris this is not.

We also discovered that it is not a wise choice to dine at restaurants serving traditional Mongolian food. It is far better to select one of the many international restaurants in town, with Chinese, Russian, and Thai the most popular.[14] Classic Mongolian cuisine has yet to discover the culinary benefits of herbs, condiments, and spices. Even Western-style grocery stores, where you can find such Americana as peanut butter and corn flakes, do not carry basil, cumin, nutmeg, or ginger. Not a drop of rosemary, sweet paprika, cinnamon, red pepper, or thyme. Empty of mustard seed, curry,

---

14. There is an excellent restaurant in town called BD's Mongolian Barbecue that serves delicious stir-fried meats and vegetables. However, it is neither Mongolian nor barbecue. It is owned by a gentleman from Ann Arbor, Michigan!

sesame, bay, and hot sauce. For seasoning, you must be content with salt and pepper, occasionally supplemented with "exotics" such as garlic and soy sauce. That's it. Mongolian cooking must surely be among the blandest and least complex cuisines on earth and, in spite of their geographic proximity and historical ties, as far removed from the spicy Szechwan dishes of Chongqing as a savory bowl of homemade Texas chili is from a can of Hormel.

During the winter, traditional Mongolian meals are composed almost exclusively of meat. Since many animals die from the unbearable cold that hovers over the country from December through March (-40 degrees is not uncommon), a nomadic Mongol family will often slaughter and eat some of its livestock during the long winter months. Since energy is essential for keeping warm, the animal's fat is highly prized, much as whale blubber is to the Inuit, and even though many Mongolians are now city dwellers and no longer nomadic, they still salivate at the thought of boiled mutton, goat, or yak, laden with thick, greasy layers of fat. When dining in a Mongolian home it would not be atypical for your meat to be resting in an inch or two of what you may think is gravy or a homemade pan sauce only to discover that it is pure liquefied animal fat.

During warmer months the Mongolian diet changes dramatically from meat to dairy. In spring the animals that survived the cold come into foal and the milk flows freely. A typical summertime meal includes freshly churned butter usually eaten with a spoon rather than spread on bread or crackers—like consuming mayonnaise directly from the jar—supplemented with other dairy products such as unpasteurized sheep's milk cheeses; dried curds; and mare's milk yogurt, extremely rich at 18 percent butterfat. Winter or summer, this is not a diet to benefit either your cholesterol or your waistline. Luckily, there was a Western-style grocery not far from our apartment that stocked fresh fruits and vegetables imported from China, allowing us to supplement this artery-hardening diet with an occasional green salad, a meal many Mongolians think is far more suited to livestock than humans.

After a few days of urban exploration it was finally time to do some work. Genghis Khan University, spelled "Chinggis Khaan" using the official Cyrillic-to-English transliteration rules, was founded in 1999 and accredited as a Mongolian institution of higher education in April 2004. It is located in a utilitarian three-story building housing forty-five faculty and eight hundred students, although there are plans to construct a new building and double the size of the student body.

I arrived early Monday morning to meet and greet the IT faculty, only to discover that none of them were there. The hallways were dark and quiet, devoid of people and academic activity. It was summer vacation, but I had assumed the computing staff would remain in town to attend my presentations. Unfortunately, that assumption was incorrect as most of the staff's parents or grandparents were nomadic farmers, and summer vacation was the only time they could visit for an extended period. Neither the entreaties of the school president nor the allure of a professional development seminar by a visiting American professor could overcome their understandable desire to see family, perhaps for the first time in many months.

In place of these seminars I volunteered to prepare a report on the current state of computer science including recommendations for its future directions. Lkhagvasuren, an anthropologist with no IT training, knew very little about the program and its curriculum while the people who did know—the computer science faculty, staff, and students—were all away from campus and not scheduled to return until after my departure.

By the end of that first day it had become clear that virtually no useful work would emerge from my visit, and I would have little, if anything, to do. Through his translator, Lkhagvasuren apologized profusely, explaining how important these home visits were to the faculty, and that scheduling my visit during the school year, rather than in the summer, would have been a far better choice. Now he tells me! I smile, accept his apology, and say that I fully understand, but as I walk back to the apartment I can only wonder what I will do to occupy my time for the next five weeks.

For the past two and a half decades our working vacation experiences played out exactly as we had hoped and expected—exotic locations affording superb attractions; high-quality schools filled with friendly staff and eager, well-qualified students; unexpectedly nice housing (with the exception of Kenya) sometimes even bordering on luxurious. The incessantly upbeat narratives of the first eleven chapters may have led you to believe that only good things happen while living and working overseas—blissfully perfect days filled with enough eye-popping adventures and fascinating stories to fill dozens of e-mails to family and friends back home.

For the last twenty-six years these rosy scenarios were a faithful and honest description of our overseas experiences. Until now. After the first few days Ruth and I knew that these five weeks in Mongolia would be a far different affair than any of our previous trips. Instead of blissfully perfect days we would struggle to stay busy in a city that had little to offer in the way of cultural, historical, architectural, or gastronomic attractions, and my work would not be a fertile source of professional satisfaction.[15]

Unfortunately, disappointment and disillusionment do occur, and when it does happen the little I can offer in terms of solace and helpful advice is *make the best of it*. When you find yourself somewhere you would rather not be, just remember that you are not out any significant financial investment (in fact, you might

---

15. An exception to this dearth of cultural attractions was the celebration of the 800th anniversary of the founding of the Mongolian Empire by Genghis Khan in 1206, an event that coincided with our visit. Special cultural shows and athletic contests were held in UB to commemorate this date. Since this happens only once every 800 years, don't expect a repeat performance when you visit.

even make a small profit), and no matter how isolated and dull the location, you should always be able to find someone or something of interest to fill your days. Just because your working vacation is not living up to expectations don't forsake any and all opportunities, no matter how small, for professional development, adventure, and plain old fun.

For example, to occupy my time at work I offered to teach a Java programming class for any students and staff remaining in town for the summer. Two people accepted this invitation and joined me in study for an hour or so each day. However, my most important contribution to the academic life and vitality of the school was bringing my wife, now a certified ESL teacher, along on the trip. Until the mid-1990s, the second language of virtually every Mongolian was Russian as the country had been a loyal ally of the Soviet Union for sixty-five years. In 1992, following the collapse of communist regimes in Eastern Europe, Mongolia had a revolution of its own leading to a new constitution and a multi-party democracy. One of the effects of this change was a headlong rush to replace Russian with English as the language of teaching, technology, commerce, and global communications, and many classes at Genghis Khan University were being taught in English even though the faculty had only a limited mastery of the tongue.

Ruth volunteered to teach an ESL course and quickly had ten people sign up, including both of my students who deserted our Java lessons as soon as they learned of this new offering. She spent many afternoons and evenings painstakingly producing materials addressing each student's particular academic needs. For example, for the three Hotel and Tourism Management faculty in her class she prepared vocabulary lists appropriate for concierge, front desk, and food service employees, and created role-playing games in which her students made reservations, ordered room service, and dealt with angry guests—all in colloquial American English.

Even though she had not planned to teach and had few materials on hand, Ruth's ESL class was so successful that by the end of our stay the students held a combination going-away/thank you/birthday party in her honor at a downtown restaurant, complete with champagne and birthday cake—both items that do not come cheaply in Mongolia. As for me, I received a thank you, a handshake, and an invitation to attend my wife's celebration.

Even though I did virtually nothing of significance during the five-week stay and was disappointed at the way things had worked out professionally, my wife ended up teaching a popular, well-received, and extremely useful ESL class for faculty and staff—something completely unplanned and unanticipated prior to arrival. When things don't work out as expected, be flexible, adjust your expectations, and do whatever you can in the time allotted. Making an unplanned contribution to an institution is far better than making no contribution at all. That's part of what making the best of it really means.

With regard to our free time, making the best of it meant escaping the concrete and cinderblock boredom of UB virtually every weekend, a common ritual for city residents. Although UB has only minimal attractions, the rural areas of the country offer much in the way of natural beauty and scenery. We were determined to fill our available free time with outdoor adventures to make up for the lack of excitement experienced during the workweek.

It is said that within the soul of every Mongolian is the desire to live a rural, nomadic lifestyle. On summer weekends and holidays this city of one million empties out as residents head to the mountains, the Gobi, or the *steppes*—those never-ending oceans of grasslands that cover half the country. Some people enjoy outdoor sports with horseback riding, fishing, and hiking the most popular. Swimming and boating are a little more difficult in a country where water temperatures rarely rise about 55 degrees, even in mid-summer.

However, organized activity is not the main purpose of these outings. Many people just sit in their *yurts*—felt covered tents—and enjoy the fresh air, endless vistas, and lack of cars, noise, and crowds. They join with family and friends in groups that may total a dozen or more, eating; drinking vodka, beer, and *ayrag* (fermented mare's milk); sharing stories; singing traditional folk songs; and experiencing a bit of the rural lifestyle their parents and/or grandparents may have led before moving to the city and leaving the nomadic life behind.

One weekend we drove with Lkhagvasuren, his wife, and Nomiko, a young female student from the school, to a *yurt* camp approximately 150 miles distant. About one hour outside the city the paved road gave way to unmarked, rutted dirt tracks criss-crossing the grasslands in what appeared to be random geometric patterns. Lkhagvasuren, who had obviously traveled the route many times, navigated this vast, empty wilderness with a smile

Typical highways of Mongolia. Which way do we go?

and an air of sureness that I took to be supreme confidence in knowing exactly where he was headed.

Fortunately, I was right. Five hours later we arrived at the camp where a dinner was to be prepared in our honor, an honor that included selecting the sheep we would eat and watching it dragged kicking and bleating from its pen, slaughtered, and gutted in front of us so we might personally appreciate its girth and fattiness. After a few too many vodka toasts and the singing of some American folksongs at our host's urging (I tried my hand at "Home, Home on the Range" and "Michael, Row the Boat Ashore"), we sat down to an extremely fresh mutton dinner. However, rather than the chops and roasts we were expecting, we dined primarily on the animal's innards—stomach, heart, liver, and intestines. These are prized delicacies and a treat we were expected to consume with relish and gusto. We consumed (and kept down) as much as we could only to see the remaining offal proudly brought to the table the following morning. Eating cold sheep intestines for breakfast exceeds even my ability to transcend cultural differences, and we were able to convince our gracious hosts that we would be quite content with toast and tea for our morning meal.

The following weekend we traveled by small propeller plane to the Gobi Desert, landing on a dirt runway that looked similar to the rutted dirt paths we had navigated by car one week earlier. Mongolians have a saying: "The Gobi is not one desert but a hundred." Unlike the Sahara, the Gobi is a crazy quilt mix of mountains, steppes, canyons, and plateaus, with only 4 percent traditional sand dunes.

On our first day in the Gobi that 4 percent was the planned destination. We set out with a driver in an old, Russian-made Jeep for an area called *Khongoryn Els*, a remote wilderness of rose-colored sand dunes, some reaching the height of a sixty-story building. The forty-mile drive from camp traversed a roadless, trackless terrain containing not a single village, not a single farm, not a single person. After about an hour the landscape changed rapidly from pancake-flat gravel plain to a rolling sea of sand rising high above the road, and the driver parked our Jeep just below one of these massive formations. We got out of the car and gazed at the uninterrupted vistas and stark beauty of the scenery—no man-made structures, no people, no animals visible anywhere. We scampered up the dune taking endless photos, enjoying the silence, and drinking in the fact that we were standing in the most sparsely populated region of the most sparsely populated country on the face of the Earth. We contemplated this utter and complete isolation until . . .

We turn around to see two men, one woman, three camels, and a dog lumbering up the dune. They seem to have materialized out of thin air. Are they rangers? (This part of the Gobi is a protected national park.) Are they part of a camel caravan to Dalanzadgad, the only town of any size in the region but still well over a hundred miles distant? Worst of all, do they intend us harm? (The driver is relaxing out of earshot at the base of the dune.)

When they reach us they dismount, smile, open the pack carried on the back of one of the camels, and proceed to set up and display their wares—an impressive collection of handmade Gobi souvenirs!

Aside from our surprise at encountering anyone in this desolate wilderness, let alone three eager entrepreneurs, we do not understand how they knew we were there. We saw no one on the drive, passed no telephone poles, certainly no WiFi "hotspots," yet somehow our appearance triggered the instant creation of this portable *tchotchke* shop. We could only laugh at imagining our being in the remotest place on Earth—possibly true, but still not too remote to conduct a little business. We haggled, bought a miniature stuffed camel for our grandson, paid for it, and smiled at them, our only common language. Once they realized we were finished buying, they bundled up their wares, loaded them onto

A portable souvenir shop in the middle of the Gobi Desert.

the pack camel, and trudged down the dune to locate other tourists who will, like us, be taken completely by surprise.

When we returned to Minneapolis after a nearly two-month sojourn I was a bit conflicted and unsure how to evaluate and reflect upon this most recent experience. At first I could not get past my unpleasant recollections of trying to offer academic guidance to a school unprepared for my arrival and a faculty seemingly uninterested in my help. And, unlike the never-ending list of five-star attractions in places like London, Jerusalem, Istanbul, Nairobi, and Kathmandu, Ulan Bator was a disappointment due to its physical unattractiveness and dearth of interesting neighborhoods, cultural institutions, and historical sites. After a dozen or so working vacations and our ritual of returning home gushing effusively over the sights we had seen and the adventures we had experienced, friends and family were surprised at our focus on those glorious two weeks in China and the subdued and muted description of our time in the *steppes* of Central Asia.

However, after a few months those unpleasant memories began to fade and the problems that once seemed so vivid and irritating became less vexing. They were slowly replaced by thoughts of the people who were so kind to us, even under difficult circumstances: Lkhagvasuren and Chujilmah, who spoke little English but nevertheless escorted us to *yurt* camps, throat-singing concerts, and traditional Mongolian restaurants; Muki, our ever-present translator, who spent hours helping us communicate instead of returning home to her husband and children; Nomiko, the young, enthusiastic university student who often joined us on out-of-town adventures and came to our apartment to practice English and discuss American culture and politics; the faculty and staff of Ruth's ESL class who were so appreciative of her efforts that they spared no expense in planning and hosting her birthday/going-away party.

I had been focusing so intently on the architectural, historical, cultural, and epicurean shortcomings of the city and country that I had overlooked the many smaller pleasures of interacting with and enjoying the company of those around me. In the long run these personal one-on-one experiences became far more important than any unpleasant meals or lack of eager students. Mongolia was a unique and completely different working vacation, one whose rewards and enjoyments came not from its physical surroundings or adventuresome offerings but from the kindness and thoughtfulness of its people.

So, ultimately, the phrase "making the most if it" might simply mean not having a predetermined and steadfast idea of exactly what makes for a great working vacation. It may mean getting past a dearth of boutique shopping, French bistros, or world-class art museums. It may mean not getting hung up over unsightly buildings, the absence of snow-capped peaks, or the lack of palm-fringed seashores. It may mean not being upset about a school not as advanced and well equipped as you may have hoped. In the end, it may simply mean becoming a more informed global citizen and enjoying the people you meet and the relationships that you form and maintain for years to come.

CHAPTER 13

The Last Shangri-La

I began this tale as a naive, unsophisticated thirty-five-year-old with no travel experience and zero global street smarts. Three decades and thirteen chapters later, I am a graying grandfather with a country count exceeding my age and a dispenser of travel advice about destinations far and wide, the great majority visited courtesy of someone else's largesse. My wife and I have gazed at Everest, ridden camels in the Gobi, walked with elephants in the Serengeti, shopped the ancient bazaars of Istanbul, and sojourned on a tropical island paradise. We've had the good fortune to live and work in Europe, the Middle East, Asia, Africa, and Oceania, all at little or no cost, and the even greater good fortune to share many of these adventures with family and friends.

I am now well into my sixth decade, retired from full-time teaching, with grandchildren to play with and spoil. You might assume this to be an age when travel tends less toward the exotic and more toward iPhoto slide shows and well-worn stories shared across the dinner table. That very reasonable assumption would be very wrong.

Retirement is exactly the time when that three- or six-month working vacation becomes an even more realistic possibility. Twenty, thirty, or even forty years of experience will have increased the size of both your résumé and reputation, and it is at this point—when you have honed your professional skills to their sharpest level—that you offer the greatest value to an international university, hospital, cultural venue, research center, or government agency. Retirement may be when you choose to stop working at home, but it is the perfect time, assuming you are healthy enough for extended travel, to start (or continue) working overseas.

Those later years are a far easier time to take a working vacation since you will not be traveling with small children and do not have to deal with such issues as primary schools, pediatricians, and playmates. But don't be surprised to find that your now *grown* children are eager to visit Mom and Dad!

Retirement affords you great flexibility in finding a mutually convenient time to take a working vacation as you are no longer constrained by temporal inconveniences such as academic calendars, research timetables, or delivery schedules. While working full time, I often found myself unable to take advantage of an international posting because my teaching schedule would not accommodate the dates when I needed to be overseas—an impediment far less vexing to those who have finished their "first" career. I can offer no better example of the benefits of flexibility and retirement-time travel than our most recent working vacation.

Chapter 7 chronicled my failure attempting to land a short-term teaching position at the Royal University of Bhutan (RUB). Following the embarrassing conclusion to those negotiations, I was momentarily tempted to write a harshly worded letter castigating their administration for the unrealistic assumption that I would travel halfway around the world and work six months without any compensation. Fortunately I calmed down, and did not. Instead, I sent a courteous thank-you note saying I was sorry things did not work out but should a position open up in the future to please keep me in mind—essentially planting a seed that, while dormant then, might someday germinate and result in an invitation. Amazingly, it did.

In summer 2009, two years after my retirement and many years after that initial failed attempt, I was home reading my e-mail when the following message suddenly appeared in the inbox:

Dear Prof Schneider,

The last time I heard from you was many years ago and a lot has happened since then. I was Dean at the Royal University of Bhutan (RUB) when you expressed interest in working there. I am now at Royal Thimphu College (RTC) and starting a new IT program. We are almost done hiring faculty for this year but have an opening and would be extremely happy to have an academician like you join us. Please let me know if you are still available and interested in working in Bhutan.

Yours sincerely,
Shivaraj Battarai, Dean
Royal Thimphu College

After recovering from my initial shock I wrote back asking for more information—I didn't want to be blindsided once again. I learned that Royal Thimphu College is a new university, just a few months old, and only the second institution of higher education in the country. The Dean, who had previously worked at RUB, remembered my earlier application, located my resume and e-mail address from the historical debris in his files, and contacted me to inquire if, after all those years, I was still interested in visiting, even for a short time. To my relief, he was not inviting me as a volunteer but as a fully paid member of the faculty. Because of the sudden resignation of one of the IT professors, he wanted me to come to RTC as soon as possible. Since I was retired and had no teaching responsibilities in the fall semester, I was able to accept his offer and began making plans to close up the house, purchase air tickets, and leave for Bhutan.

Due to unexpected illnesses, impending deadlines, last-minute resignations, or larger-than-anticipated enrollments, this type of "I need you ASAP" invitation from an overseas institution is not all that unusual, and it is exactly the kind of offer that meshes so well with the scheduling flexibility afforded by retirement. I doubt whether many fully employed professionals could, on such short notice, walk away from their current positions and head off to the other side of the globe.

Americans and Europeans know very little about Bhutan, which is not surprising given that it was one of the most isolated countries in the world and effectively closed to Western visitors and journalists until the late 1960s. The first scheduled international airline flight into the country was in 1988, while cell phones, cable TV, and the Internet did not arrive until 1999.

Bhutan is now open to both tourism and the international media, and in its wake the nation is struggling to maintain a balance between its ancient traditions and bringing the benefits of globalization and modernization to its populace. On one hand, Mahayana Buddhism permeates all aspects of personal behavior and daily life. The killing of animals is strictly forbidden—the reason for the large number of stray dogs wandering the streets. Citizens are required to adhere to the *Driglam Namzha,* the official dress code dating to the seventeenth century, and wear traditional clothing—the *gho* for men, *kira* for women—at work, school, and government offices. All public buildings are constructed in the Bhutanese *dzong* architectural style, and schools still teach the "Thirteen Traditional Arts and Crafts" which trace their roots to the fifteenth century. At the same time, though, my apartment had

WiFi access, the government had just completed the first four-lane expressway, upscale coffee shops were sprouting on urban street corners, and a modern, 18-hole golf course was being constructed in the capital.

This lurch toward modernization is being guided by the principle of *Gross National Happiness (GNH)*, first postulated by Jigme Singye Wangchuck, the fourth King of Bhutan, in 1972.[16] It attempts to measure a nation's quality of life using not just income data, trade balances, and the manufacture of material goods but also individual well being, moral and ethical ideals, and Buddhist spiritual values. Every development project is judged not only on how much money it might generate but also by the benefits— educational, physical, medical, and environmental—it will bring to its citizens. This holistic view of society is rare on a continent where most governments worship the deity of unconstrained economic growth, and politicians care far more about personal gain than national happiness.

Western tourism to Bhutan, while permitted, is closely regulated, and independent travel is prohibited except for reasons of employment. You must arrive with an authorized tour group and spend a minimum of $250 per person per day, a cost that limits most visitors to a brief seven- to fourteen-day stay, hardly enough time to learn about and appreciate the beauty and complexity of this rapidly evolving society—yet another demonstration of the benefits of a long-term working vacation.

In late September 2009, only two months after receiving that first e-mail, Ruth and I walked out the front door of our home, leaving our property in the care of neighbors, and departed Minneapolis for a two-month stay in the hauntingly beautiful Himalayan

---

16. For an interesting discussion of Gross National Happiness check out "Recalculating Happiness in a Himalayan Kingdom," by Seth Mydans, in the *New York Times,* May 6, 2009.

kingdom of Bhutan—Land of the Thunder Dragon and the last Shangri-La. Twenty-nine years after nervously exiting the plane in London, England, my wife and I set off on our fourteenth working vacation, eager to learn about and become part of this unique thirteen-hundred-year-old Buddhist society.

We were met at the airport by a university van and driven thirty miles to the campus of Royal Thimphu College (RTC) and our lovely two-bedroom faculty apartment. The school is set on twenty-five acres of pine forest at an altitude of 8,500 feet, with snow-capped Himalayan peaks ringing the horizon. While located in a pristine, invigorating alpine location, the college is only a fifteen-minute drive from Thimphu, the bustling capital city, via the nation's first high-speed expressway.

After unpacking and settling in, we picked up our rental car, a tiny, well-worn five-year-old subcompact. When I had learned that RTC was six miles from the city center with bus service limited to early morning and late afternoon hours, mostly to provide access for staff living in Thimphu, I followed my own advice and sent e-mail to every school employee announcing that I was in the market for a private, two-month rental. I was able to connect with a college administrator who owned two cars and saw an opportunity to generate some income from the older one that sat unused most of the day. The $200/month cost was far below the rate of commercial firms, and it afforded Ruth and me the freedom to drive into the city at our convenience as well as tour the countryside on days that I was not teaching—although it was a struggle for our little Maruti, with its three cylinder 37 horsepower engine, to conquer those 12,000 foot Bhutanese mountain passes. But it managed.

Most of the RTC faculty is international, the majority coming from India but with a smattering of Brits and Americans, including a retired anthropology professor from Carleton College in Northfield, Minnesota, only thirty-five miles from our home!

These individuals were delightful, interesting and adventurous, and they became close friends with whom we traveled, trekked, and dined.

However, to avoid falling into the "expat trap" described in Chapter 9, Ruth and I were also eager to make friends with local Bhutanese. I again followed my own advice and, before leaving home, contacted the Alumni Office to see if there were any Macalester graduates living in Bhutan. There was one—Dechen Roder, a young Bhutanese woman from the class of '03, who enthusiastically responded to my request to meet for coffee at a downtown Thimphu café. It turned out to be a fortuitous connection as she was not only fun to spend time with but also politically active, and she opened our eyes to some of the thorny social and economic issues currently facing her country.

She introduced us to her boyfriend, Pema, a skilled painter who took us on a tour of VAST, the Volunteer Artists Studio of Thimphu. VAST is a cooperative guild founded in 1998 to help nurture and support young Bhutanese artists who want to experiment with genres other than classical Buddhist *thangka* paintings, the traditional style taught in most art schools.

We also spent time with Dechen's mother, Kunzang Choden, one of Bhutan's most well known writers and the author of *Dawa: The Story of a Stray Dog in Bhutan*[17] and *The Circle of Karma*.[18] Prior to our departure from the United States, a good friend who travels frequently in South Asia loaned us these books to give us a better understanding of Bhutanese history and culture, totally unaware of the author's connection to the Twin Cities. We ended up purchasing our own copies for Kunzang to autograph, and they are among the most prized "souvenirs" of our visit.

---

17. Kunzang Choden, *Dawa: The Story of a Stray Dog in Bhutan,* 2nd ed., (n.p.: KMT Press, 2006).

18. Kunzang Choden, *The Circle of Karma,* (n.p.: Penguin Global, 2005).

We became good friends with the RTC Dean, Shivaraj, his wife Tulsa who was a teacher at a local elementary school, and their two sons—Suraj, a twenty-two-year-old computer scientist, and Arun, a twenty-four-year-old documentary filmmaker with the Bhutanese Broadcasting System—and we often joined them for meals and conversation during our stay.

The Choden family and the Battarais were invaluable resources in helping us learn about the country's history, politics, and culture as well as the rapidly changing nature of urban Bhutanese life in the twenty-first century. While Ruth and I enjoyed and appreciated our friendships with the American, English, and Indian faculty of RTC, they were, like us, recently arrived international visitors. It was through our relationship with locals like Dechen, Pema, Kunzang, Shivaraj, Tulsa, and others that we began to understand and appreciate life in this remote Himalayan kingdom.

I taught four days a week, Monday through Thursday, but Tuesday and Thursday were my busiest days when I would leave for school in the early morning and not return to the apartment until late afternoon or evening. To keep from getting bored on those two days, Ruth offered to assist Tulsa in her fifth-grade classroom with its forty-two students—a handful for any teacher. She taught units on English spelling, grammar, and literature, and joined the class for field trips around the city, including attendance at "National Hand Washing Day," an integral part of the country's effort to minimize the spread of the potentially deadly H1N1 virus, a comprehensive plan developed immediately after discovery of the first confirmed case just a few months earlier.

Even though we were in the country for only two months, Ruth was able to contribute to a local elementary school, share ideas and techniques with teachers, and observe the approach to elementary education in Bhutan. No matter how short your visit, there are always useful volunteer opportunities for the non-working spouse. All you need to do is put a little effort into finding them.

On Friday, Saturday, and Sunday, Ruth and I would hop into our little red Maruti and head out to see some of the many five-star sights described in the travel guides. This included a visit to the *Taktsang* monastery, Tiger's Nest in English, a name derived from the legend that Guru Rinpoche, the Indian sage who brought Buddhism to Bhutan in the eighth century, flew to this remote site on the back of a magic tiger. The monastery, the most famous in the country, sits at an altitude of 10,200 feet and is perched on the edge of a cliff a dizzying half mile above the valley floor. After parking your car, you can either walk the 2,500-foot vertical rise along a steep, dirt path or opt for a donkey. Foolishly we chose to go it on foot, a choice I came to regret as we slowly trudged up the last few hundred feet. While retirement may be the ideal time to take a working vacation, it is also the ideal time to admit your age and accept whatever assistance is offered.

On all these trips around the country we did not book our reservations until after we had arrived. Because of my teaching

The Tiger's Nest Monestary in Bhutan.

contract with RTC, I was issued a Bhutanese ID card indicating I was in the country as an employee, not as a tourist. This entitled Ruth and me to discounts at museums, historical sites, and national parks, as well as reduced rates on guides and hotel rooms— discounts I would not have received if these items had been purchased online in the United States. This confirmed my earlier suggestion that it is usually better to wait until you arrive to purchase your accommodations, tours, and transportation tickets.

In addition to the biggies of Bhutanese tourism, such as Tiger's Nest, we also received excellent advice from locals about off-the-beaten-track adventures not included in the Lonely Planet and virtually untouched by tourists during their seven- or ten-day whirlwind visit. One such piece of advice resulted in the most unusual experience we had during our two-month stay.

The Nalanda Buddhist Institute is a 250-year-old monastery and school. It is located on a remote mountainside about a three-hour drive from the capital. There are 180 monks living at Nalanda, ranging in age from eight to twenty-five, and in addition to their religious studies the institute provides each student with English lessons. There are language classes twice a day, six days a week, and the school eagerly welcomes native speakers to help the monks, especially the younger ones, improve their conversational skills. In exchange for teaching two ninety-minute classes the monastery will provide a room, all meals, and an introduction to the basics of monastic life, a lifestyle about which Ruth and I were completely ignorant. It sounded like an ideal opportunity and exactly the kind of unique experience that distinguishes travelers from casual tourists. We immediately called the head monk and booked our reservations.

As we made the winding seventy-mile drive from Thimphu, I thought about what our accommodations might look like. Having seen too many Hollywood movies like "Seven Years in Tibet," I imagined sleeping on straw mats in a bare room lit only by candlelight, with meals consisting of peasant bread and weak soup taken in solitude and contemplation. Fortunately, these overwrought images were totally incorrect as our room was quite pleasant and the food was both plentiful and delicious.

Our only concern was the bathroom, located one hundred feet from the sleeping quarters on the edge of a steep cliff. While not posing a problem during the day, at our age night bathroom runs are a routine occurrence. As a male I could relieve myself just about anywhere, but Ruth insisted on waking me up and tightly clutching my arm as we haltingly made our way along that perilous path guided only by the light of my keychain flashlight. When we arrived at the outhouse I would stand guard outside since there was only a single facility—not surprising given that Nalanda housed 180 men and no women.

For our English classes the monks were divided into two groups, the younger ones aged eight to thirteen and the older ones ranging from fourteen to the mid-twenties. For my first class I had the younger ones. Since, unlike my wife, I am not a trained ESL teacher, I decided that instead of grammar and vocabulary lessons we would have a pleasant conversation about anything that interested them in order to practice listening to and talking with a native English speaker, albeit a native speaker with a thick East Coast accent courtesy of my parents' New Jersey heritage.

Although my students were studying sacred Buddhist scriptures and were dressed in the classic monk garb they were also young, immature pre-adolescents so their questions were mostly of the form "Do you listen to Michael Jackson?" or "What's your favorite sport?" It appears that ten-year-olds, even those wearing saffron-colored robes, are pretty much the same world over.

The next day Ruth and I switched groups. I now had the older monks, and our discussions took a noticeable turn. Their curiosity ran more toward Barack Obama, democracy (which did not arrive in Bhutan until March 2008), and my Judaism, a religion

My wife Ruth teaching the Buddhist monks of Nalanda.

they knew absolutely nothing about. Buddhism is not based on worship of a Supreme Being and belief in an afterlife but on studying the teachings of Buddha, leading an ethical life, and achieving a state of enlightenment. To learn about Judaism they did not ask me such obvious questions as "Do you believe in God?" but instead presented me with moral dilemmas such as "What would your religion tell you to do if someone killed your wife?" I felt like a rabbi-in-training during an oral examination. The class became less of an English lesson and more of a debate about moral and ethical behavior, a debate in which I was definitely overmatched.

Our two months in Bhutan raced by far more quickly than we wanted, and Ruth and I wholeheartedly agreed that this was one of the most intellectually stimulating and enjoyable working vacations of our traveling lives. The country boasts friendly people, fresh mountain air, spectacular scenery, great tourist sights, a rich quality of life, and a fascinating Buddhist culture. Our last few days in the country included the familiar round of going-away parties and good-bye hugs. The Dean and Director invited me to return to RTC following my regular spring-semester stint at Columbia, an invitation I am mulling over as I weigh the trade-offs between the "repeater" and "not-again" schools of working-vacation travel.

On our return to the United States we added a four-day visit to the northern Indian state of Sikkim, a lightly visited but beautiful region of the country recommended to us by our Bhutanese friends. This four-day stopover added only a modest fee to our airline ticket, and we were able to make arrangements at a very reasonable cost, through a local Thimphu travel agency, for ground transport, hotel rooms, and tour guides.

This working vacation in Bhutan turned out to be a rousing confirmation of many of the travel suggestions presented in this book: 1) contacting individuals to arrange a private automobile rental, 2) arranging for the non-working spouse to perform volunteer work to stay active and involved, 3) using your HR office or Alumni Center to meet locals, 4) not purchasing tours or hotel rooms in advance of arrival, 5) using the advice and counsel of locals to identify unique and interesting side trips, and 6) turning your air ticket into a "twofer" by adding a second stopover on the way there or back. All of these ideas were put to successful use during our two months in the Himalayas.

The trip was also confirmation that, even though my wife and I are both retired and well into our sixties, it is certainly not too late to consider living and working overseas. (Remember, though, choose the donkey!) In the coming years, until my aging body rebels and says "No more," I hope to take additional working vacations and add many new chapters to future editions of this book.

Chapter 7, which chronicled my working-vacation failures,

closed with the inspirational words "If you keep trying, and sometimes trying and trying and trying, good things can happen. Just remember that failure is simply one step in the overall process, not the final outcome." For some readers these lofty words may ring hollow and be seen as nothing more than a literary attempt to tell a good story and sell a few books.

I trust this penultimate chapter will put that cynicism to rest and inspire you to keep trying for your dream working vacation even after receiving that initial "We are so sorry but . . ." response. Like this unexpected trip to Bhutan, good things really can happen when you are firmly committed to living and working overseas and dedicated to the idea of learning from, contributing to, and integrating into a new culture.

Sow those travel seeds and be diligent, persistent, and, most important, patient in going after any and all opportunities that will allow you to achieve this goal.

CHAPTER 14

It's Your Turn Now

One of the many facts gleaned from my three decades of travel is that it is impossible to comprehensively catalog the many different ways of unearthing good working-vacation opportunities. Previous chapters described techniques that have worked well for me—contacts made at professional conferences, articles in journals and trade magazines, cold calls to department chairs, the advice of other professionals, and federal and foundation travel grants. However, this list is far from complete and the past few years have opened my eyes to possibilities I had never previously considered. Locating good working vacations is a skill one never stops improving, regardless of how long you have been doing it.

For example, I was invited to lead a Macalester College Alumni Association eighteen-day safari to Kenya and Tanzania, with all air and land costs covered by the college. Before being contacted by the alumni office staff I never knew such tours existed or that faculty members were asked to lead them. My invitation to be a tour leader was not due to any extensive background in African history, geography, or culture—although I did spend two working vacations on the African continent—but the far more prosaic fact that the trip is scheduled for late October and early November when most of my non-retired colleagues will be hard at work in the library, classroom, and laboratory.

A few months ago I was contacted by the Dean of Multimedia University in Malaysia where I spent seven months as a Fulbright Scholar, an experience described in Chapter 10. His e-mail asked if I would be willing to accept a three-year appointment as an "External Examiner" in the Faculty of Information Technology. I did not reply immediately even though I am not one to turn down an overseas invitation; I simply had no clue what an external examiner was or did. After searching online I discovered it to be an artifact of the British system of higher education that is still used in countries whose universities follow the British model, a list that includes Malaysia. An external examiner is someone not affiliated with the school who reviews and approves final examinations before they are administered to ensure that grading standards are reasonable and examination questions are appropriate for the course level and time allotted.

In addition to reviewing examinations, an external examiner is invited to visit the campus once during a three-year appointment, at the school's expense, to evaluate the educational program and make recommendations for improvement. Essentially, I am required to accept a free trip to Malaysia! That sold me, and I immediately e-mailed back an affirmative response. Sometime in the next three years, yours truly and spouse will return to Southeast Asia for a bit of work with, undoubtedly, some interesting detours added to the return trip itinerary—all for a position that I had to look up in Wikipedia to discover what it was and what I was supposed to do!

Our two grown children live and work in New York City, a long commute from our permanent home in Minneapolis. My wife and I thought it would be fun to live at least part of the year in

New York, after retirement, to be closer to our children and grand-children, a closeness that grows in importance as one ages. It was then that I discovered another great working vacation option—visiting professorships.

It is a well-known dirty secret of academia that tenured faculty at prestigious research universities will do anything they can to avoid teaching large, introductory freshman/sophomore lecture classes. Such "menial duties" are usually dumped in the laps of graduate students, part-time adjuncts, or visiting professors—often retired academics and professionals like me. I contacted Columbia University about the possibility of a visiting position; submitted a résumé, letters of recommendation, and teaching evaluations; was interviewed by the department chair; and am now a Visiting Professor of Computer Science at Columbia teaching one class every spring semester for as long as I wish.[19] Not only do I earn a decent salary teaching this class, but I also qualify to live in a luxurious college-owned and college-subsidized faculty apartment (three bedrooms/three baths/1,700 square feet/doorman) at a price so deeply discounted that it might not cover the monthly rent of a tiny, market-rate one-bedroom. Columbia might not be an "overseas" position, but it definitely qualifies as a no-cost working vacation, a pleasant surprise given that New York is one of the most expensive cities in the world.

The residents of the apartment we sublet are New York University faculty (Columbia professors are permitted to sublet in NYU-owned buildings) residing in Florence, Italy for six months while heading the "NYU in Florence Program," an example of yet another interesting working-vacation possibility. Many campuses, or

---

19. I selected Columbia rather than NYU when I learned, to my surprise, that Columbia uses my textbook in one of its courses. While that was no doubt helpful, it is not necessary to have a prior association with a school to be appointed to a visiting position; you need good professional qualifications and experience.

associations of campuses, have overseas study programs or joint operating agreements with international schools. Faculty from the U.S. campus are typically appointed for one or two semesters to supervise students and teach courses at the overseas branch—not a bad gig when that branch is in London, Paris, or Florence.

For example, Macalester is a member of the Associated Colleges of the Midwest (ACM), a consortium of thirteen liberal arts colleges in Illinois, Iowa, Minnesota, Wisconsin, and Colorado. The ACM offers study-away programs in Britain, Botswana, Brazil, Costa Rica, India, Italy, Japan, and Mexico, and it appoints a Faculty Director, paid a regular college salary, from one of the member colleges to travel with students, handle any problems that arise, and teach courses for one semester. I have not yet investigated this opportunity but it is certainly on my short list, especially since my scheduling flexibility could make me a highly attractive candidate.

What some might cynically call the ultimate boondoggle is the Semester at Sea program, www.semesteratsea.org, which has been in existence since 1926 and is operated under the academic sponsorship of the University of Virginia. This floating college runs voyages in fall, spring, and summer semesters (each lasting roughly three to four months), includes ten to twelve ports of call, and provides twelve to fifteen college credits for each of its undergraduate "sailors." Approximately thirty faculty and thirty staff members are selected for each voyage through an application process that reviews teaching or professional work experience, field of expertise, and familiarity with at least one of the countries where the ship will be stopping.

In exchange for carrying out administrative work or teaching two to three classes, successful applicants receive a salary as well as full room and board. A voyage aboard the *MV Explorer* may include visits to Cadiz, Spain; Casablanca, Morocco; Tema/Accra,

Ghana; Cape Town, South Africa; Port Louis, Mauritius; Chennai, India; Ho Chi Minh City, Viet Nam; Hong Kong/Shanghai, China; Singapore; Kobe/Yokohama Japan; and Honolulu/Hilo, Hawaii. Not a bad way to see the world while earning a salary and having your food and lodging expenses fully covered.

I've spent the first thirteen chapters of this book describing how I was able to locate overseas working vacations and then, in just the last few paragraphs, I added five more possibilities—alumni tours, external examiners, visiting professorships, study-away directors, and Semester at Sea. Why this piecemeal approach? Why don't I just list, in step-by-step fashion, exactly what you must do and where you must go to locate the best overseas opportunities in your field? Instead of this travel memoir, why not simply write an instructional how-to guide entitled *Working Vacations for Dummies?*

Unfortunately, that highly appealing idea is totally unrealistic. Volatility is the nature of this beast with new working-vacation possibilities continually being created and unexpected opportunities constantly popping up on the radar. Furthermore, professionals in such diverse fields as dentistry, architecture, pharmacy, and dance could easily add dozens of suggestions specific to their own disciplines.

Given the almost unlimited number of places to search and possibilities to explore, the best advice I can give to any potential traveler is *be alert for any working-vacation opportunity no matter where it may appear, how you may have found it, or how it may have found you.* I would have loved to end this book with hundreds of Web sites containing working-vacation prospects neatly sorted by country and field of specialization—one click and you are on your way—but that scenario is not a possibility since each specialization will have its own unique assortment of foundations, grants, agencies, and programs. A technique that works well for the computer science professor may not work equally as well for the surgeon. Opportunities open to a concert violinist will be meaningless to the nuclear physicist.

Even though I cannot exhaustively list all the places you should look and all the techniques you should try, I hope reading about my experiences has made you so eager to live and work overseas that you are willing to search out any and all opportunities in your field and work aggressively to turn those possibilities into reality. The real trick to creating a working vacation is not so much knowing exactly where to look but knowing exactly how to respond when an exciting travel/work opportunity presents itself.

In spite of this somewhat mixed message, I can provide at least a few pointers to helpful online sites to get you started on your search. Following are some useful Web sites you might wish to investigate.

- www.cies.org

The best place to start your search is the Fulbright Scholar site sponsored by the U.S. State Department's Bureau of Educational and Cultural Affairs and administered by the Council for the International Exchange of Scholars (CIES). Even though this book was written from the perspective of a college teacher, Fulbrighters are, in the words of their Web site, "teachers, administrators, lawyers, doctors, business people, artists, photographers, and other independent scholars." Each year CIES sends 800 or more U.S. professionals off to every corner of the globe and, even though I was the lucky recipient of four, the great majority of grantees are newcomers; last year 87 percent of grant recipients were first-timers. This site will point you to information about how to apply for either a traditional Fulbright Scholar Grant or the short-term Senior Specialist Award. It also contains news about special programs; tips for writing a successful application; and a place to sign up to receive the *Global Citizen,* the monthly newsletter of the

Fulbright Foundation, which will keep you informed about new grant opportunities.

- www.bravenewtraveler.com/2007/08/29/the-complete-guide-to-finding-winning-travel-grants/

If you decide to write a Fulbright grant, or any other federal or foundation travel grant, before putting pen to paper you might wish to check out this Web site, entitled *The Complete Guide To Finding & Winning Travel Grants.* The author, Preethi Burkholder, is a professional grant writer and author of ten books about travel and grantsmanship. She provides excellent tips on researching funding agencies, evaluating potential travel grants, avoiding some of the most common mistakes, and preparing your application. It is an invaluable resource for information about writing travel grants.

- www.transitionsabroad.com

This is a comprehensive portal for all types of resources about living, working, and studying abroad. The site is sponsored by *Transitions Abroad* magazine founded in 1977 by Dr. Clay Hubbs, a professor and study-away advisor at Hampshire College. The magazine's goal is to provide "information enabling travelers to meet the people of other countries, learn about their culture, speak their language, and 'transition' to a new level of understanding and appreciation for our fascinating world." It has grown from a single journal into a collection of print and electronic publications, including travel books such as *Work Abroad: The Complete Guide to Finding a Job Overseas,*[20] and *Alternative Travel*

---

20. Clayton A. Hubbs, ed., *Work Abroad: The Complete Guide to Finding a Job Overseas 4th ed.,* (n.p.: Transitions Abroad, 2002).

Directory: The Complete Guide to Traveling, Studying & Living Overseas;[21] a monthly webzine, *TAzine*; and the award-winning www.transitionsabroad.com Web site. The portal includes links to all these resources as well as lists of short-term employment possibilities, international teaching positions, overseas internships, study abroad, and volunteer work.

- www.state.gov/m/dghr/flo/c21946.htm

This U.S. State Department page, entitled "Teaching Overseas," contains links to K-12 and college-level overseas teaching opportunities. It includes resources for locating positions, procedures for making initial contact with local schools, listings of teaching positions at American schools overseas as well as schools operated on behalf of dependents of Department of Defense employees, and information about the Teacher Exchange Program sponsored by the Fulbright Foundation.

- www.go-defense.com/

In the words of the Careers in National Defense Web site, "it takes more than soldiers to protect America." The site includes listings of civilian jobs, from entry level to executive, in every state of the union as well as dozens of foreign countries. It has a handy, easy-to-use search engine, jobsearch.godefense.newjobs. com, which allows you to select an individual country and see what positions are currently available there. For example, a search using the keyword "Italy" produced a listing of 141 opportunities in law, information technology, quality assurance, security, child

---

21. Bill Nolting, *Alternative Travel Directory: The Complete Guide to Traveling, Studying & Living Overseas,* 7th ed., ed. Ron Mader (n.p.: Transitions Abroad, 2002).

development, management, architecture, and natural resources. (It even included three openings for bartenders!) The site also allows you to search the database by field of specialization rather than location, with hundreds of possibilities ranging from accountant to zoologist, including such unexpected ones as archeologist, baker, historian, and locksmith.

• federaljobs.net/overseas.htm

This Web site, not affiliated with the U.S. government, is dedicated to helping people locate federal job opportunities with the Department of Defense, the largest employer of U.S. citizens with 50,000 overseas civilian employees. It describes the conditions of employment, the application process for federal overseas work, and links to the employment Web sites of the U.S. Army, Navy, Air Force, and Marines.

• www.doctorswithoutborders.org/work/field/

Doctors Without Borders/Médecins Sans Frontières (MSF) was founded in 1971, in France, and is one of the largest sources of overseas work opportunities for those working in the fields of medicine and public health. The agency currently operates in nearly sixty countries, and was awarded the Nobel Peace Prize in 1999. Doctors Without Borders recruits professionals—including doctors, osteopaths, nurses, midwives, pharmacists, clinical psychologists, and laboratory technicians—for periods of nine to twelve months to work in a wide range of fields. MSF also recruits non-medical professionals in related areas such as health administration, health economics, water and sanitation engineering, and epidemiology. Positions include a monthly salary, per diem living allowance, round-trip transportation, in-country room and board, and comprehensive medical and life insurance.

- www.jobsabroad.com/search.cfm

This site advertises: "Wouldn't it be nice if your vacation paid for itself? What you need are short-term positions, and here's where to find them." It then provides a search mechanism that allows you to select either the country where you wish to work or the type of work you would like to find. Like many similar sites, the jobs listed are often introductory positions geared more toward young, single college graduates than mature professionals— jobs such as teaching English, working in food service industries, or being an au pair. However, the site does include some professional positions (e.g., in computer science it lists positions for Web page designers and software developers), so it is worth your time and effort to check it out.

- www.women-on-the-road.com/overseas-jobs.html

This site is dedicated to providing helpful information to women who love to travel on their own and live and work overseas, although most of the information is not gender specific and anyone can benefit from its excellent advice and counsel. It has a particularly useful section on locating overseas positions with nonprofit organizations such as Oxfam, International Red Cross, and the United Nations. The site also includes stories submitted by readers who have followed its advice and obtained interesting overseas work, such as a cruise ship youth counselor, professional storyteller, flower arranger, and even a milkmaid on a French goat farm!

- www.globalvolunteers.org/maps/world_map.asp
- www.serviceleader.org/new/international/articles/
  2004/03/000211.php

This book has focused on paid professional positions that allow you to enjoy a high-level working vacation while someone else picks up the tab. There is a socially responsible alternative called "volunteer tourism" in which you contribute important services in your field of expertise to impoverished communities at no cost to the host country. Typically, you spend two to three weeks overseas and are responsible for your own transportation. In addition, the private non-profit agency that arranges the position will usually charge a service fee that can range from a few hundred to a few thousand dollars, depending on destination and length of stay. This service fee covers the cost of your orientation program, in-country support, living accommodations, and some meals.

Global Volunteers, founded in 1984, is one of the largest such organizations with 2,500 volunteers currently working overseas in nineteen countries. ServiceLeader.org is a project of the Lyndon B. Johnson School of Public Affairs at the University of Texas at Austin, and its goal is to provide information about all aspects of volunteerism. The URL above contains a list of Web sites with information about overseas service-learning opportunities lasting from one week to several years.

My friends often refer to my wife and me as "lucky" or "special," and comment that we appear to be leading an ideal life that allows us to travel the world, live among different cultures, experience strange and unique adventures, and see sights that most people are limited to viewing on the Discovery channel or reading about in *National Geographic.* I trust this book has made two things very clear—it was not "luck" that led me to this lifestyle, and I am not a particularly "special" person in terms of employment, skills, or abilities. What I am, though, is thoroughly committed to tracking down working vacation opportunities, and totally dedicated to taking full advantage of these opportunities whenever and wherever they occur.

It was not luck that got me to Israel but my dedication to turn a small, relatively insignificant newspaper article into a no-cost overseas experience. It was not luck that sent me to Kenya, Turkey, and Zimbabwe, but a willingness to make cold calls to department chairs offering my services as a visiting professor. It was not luck that allowed me to live in Mauritius and Malaysia, but my readiness to spend time searching the Fulbright *Catalog of Awards* and filling out the Fulbright application form. It was not luck that took me to Nepal or Mongolia, but my commitment to contact the dean or computer science head at overseas schools, explain the Senior Specialist program, and convince him to apply for a grant to support my visit. And it was not luck that finally got me to Bhutan but my perseverance in planting dozens of "travel seeds" in countries around the world in the hope that someday one of them would sprout into a fascinating, no-cost working vacation, which is exactly what happened.

One fact that has become clear to me after all these overseas trips is that there is no shortage of working vacation opportunities, only a shortage of the motivation needed to go after them. I hope my stories and advice will motivate you to consider applying for a working vacation of your own. Reading someone else's adventure stories may be a pleasant diversion, but it is nothing like the thrill of experiencing those same adventures for yourself.

As mentioned in the opening pages of the book, it is easy to come up with dozens of reasons why you and your family cannot travel right now and must put it off until next year, or the year after that, or . . . In response I offer the following counter-argument: In the future I want *you,* not me, to be the one others look at, admire, and say to, "You are a very lucky and a very special person." I want *you,* not me, to be the one who sends e-mail and photos to friends and family back home from places they can only dream of visiting. I want *you,* not me, to be the one who travels the world, lives among different cultures, and has exotic adventures—all on the other guy's dime.

Theodore Geisel, aka Dr. Seuss, the beloved children's author read and enjoyed throughout the world, captured this idea far better than I could ever hope to:

> You have brains in your head.
> You have feet in your shoes.
> You can steer yourself any direction you choose.
> You're on your own. And you know what you know.
> And YOU are the guy who'll decide where to go.
> . . . .
> And will you succeed?
> Yes! You will, indeed.
> (98 and ¾ percent guaranteed.)[22]

And please, send me some e-mail when you arrive.

---

22. Dr. Seuss, *Oh, the Places You'll Go!* (New York: Random House, 1990).

Acknowledgements

There are many people I wish to thank for helping to bring this project to fruition. First of all let me say thank you to my son Benjamin, my daughter Rebecca, and my son-in-law Trevor. When I retired their gift to me was a travel writing class at the Gotham Writer's Workshop in New York City, a class that inspired me to begin writing this book. More accurately, it was the instructor, Mr. Kurt Oprecht, himself a gifted and talented author, who kindled in me a passion for story telling.

My editor, Ms. Beverly Ehrman, a Picasso with a red pen, then turned that rough draft into a finished and polished document. I have one piece of advice for all budding authors–no matter how good a writer you are and no matter how interesting your ideas may be, a skilled editor can greatly improve how those ideas are expressed, an improvement that Bev certainly achieved.

It does no good to produce a finished manuscript if no one reads it. I owe a huge debt of gratitude to my agent, Mr. Bill Hammond of the 2Bills Literary Agency, who formed the team that turned this manuscript into a finished product. That includes Don Leeper and Rachel Holscher of BookMobile Inc. who were responsible for design and printing, and Mark Jung of Itasca Books, who handled publishing and distribution. Finally, a big thanks to my publicist, Bonnie Harris of Wax Marketing Inc., for helping me to reach those individuals who could benefit from the advice and suggestions contained in these pages. This is an extremely talented group of professionals.

And last, but most certainly not least, a big hug and thank you to my wife Ruthann, who is not only my travel partner but my life partner and best friend as well. Without her there would be no story at all.